THE TRUE S...
RAMRAIDERS
CRASH N
CARRY

THE TRUE STORY OF BRITAIN'S
RAMRAIDERS
CRASH N CARRY

STEPHEN RICHARDS
FOREWORD BY FREDDIE FOREMAN

JOHN BLAKE

Published by John Blake Publishing Ltd,
3 Bramber Court, 2 Bramber Road,
London W14 9PB, England

www.blake.co.uk

First published in paperback in 2005

ISBN 1 84454 106 1

British Library Cataloguing-in-Publication Data:

A catalogue record for this book is available from the British Library.

Design by www.envydesign.co.uk

Printed in Great Britain by BookMarque

1 3 5 7 9 10 8 6 4 2

Papers used by John Blake Publishing are natural, recyclable
products made from wood grown in sustainable forests.
The manufacturing processes conform to the environmental
regulations of the country of origin.

Every attempt has been made to contact the relevant copyright-holders,
but some were unobtainable. We would be grateful if the appropriate
people could contact us.

For the late, beloved James Ravenscroft,
a man we should all aspire to be like

Dale and Colin

On a dark and bleak winter's night
two stars shine bright
Beacons, leading the way, guiding
us so as to steer away

I have seen the light, how it made my eyes bleed
with tears of sadness at such a loss in a dire tragic
manner, so needlessly they were driven on, 'They were
the best', shouted the voices from afar, Oh yeah!
How would you like to fucking die in a
burning mangled car?

Both were artists from your time, living in times
of hardship that demanded you change your Nikes for
Armani for Le Coq for something better.

The chasing blue light seemed so far behind,
but freedom was all they had in mind, a straight
road was so unkind

Some say they saw contact made, but with what
no one really knows. The police car was covered with
what might have been a grim reaper's cape, but in
reality it was a dirty old tarpaulin – that's all what
the media seen.

CONTENTS

FOREWORD

I GUESS YOU could say I am the original 'Ramraider'. My first experience of car-related crime was when I was a youngster. We'd follow a travelling salesman and as soon as he went into the house, selling goods on the never-never, the jump-up would happen. You'd use a screwdriver to open the quarterlight window of his motor, up went the catch, open the door and start the car up with a flat key (a Lucas key) and drive off. OK, it wasn't the crime of the century – that was to come later, but it was the beginning.

We didn't have fancy four-wheel-drive Jeeps at our disposal in the ramraid game. I was always looking for something new to do in my move up the ladder. As I grew older I was continuously on the lookout for more ambitious projects. On one of our shopping expeditions, shortly before Christmas, we found a store in Clapham Junction, which could easily be burgled by tampering with its steel shutters. It was an ideal night for the robbery because a thick fog had blanketed London. I had already borrowed a large van from a market guy in Covent Garden and told him to scream if anything went wrong, otherwise we'd return the van the following day.

Everything went to plan. We got to the store that night, up came the shutters and in we went while the night watchman was fast asleep in his office. In no time at all we took what we wanted and had the pick of each department: washing machines, carpets, vacuum cleaners, curtains. We began loading up the van and, just as we finished loading, a guy came walking out of the fog so we decided to move – fast. I stayed in the van to finish packing and no sooner had I done this than a law car pulled up with its wheels screeching. It stopped bang in front of me. It had come on top and there was only one thing for it, but the cossers piled out and got a hold of me.

I struggled and came clean out of my jacket, and I made my way through the fog. I hid underneath a car covered with a canvas. I got away with it. I was young and fit and could get away with an awful lot – and I did. Knowing of the exploits that follow in this book, I know I led the way. We entered premises while security guards were on patrol, just like these ramraiders did.

The car was a good tool and we used it as if it was specifically designed for the job of ramraiding. I was grafting with a guy called Joe Carter one time. Joey and I used to do the windows: smash them and grab all the gear in the early hours of the morning. You'd either reverse the car into the window or you smashed it with a heavy object.

One night we were involved in a terrible chase around Streatham. There were about three patrol cars in front and another three behind when police cordoned off the road and made us stop. As they approached the car we took off again like something out of Brands Hatch, crashing patrol cars as we escaped. They gave chase because they knew we'd been grafting the area and had been waiting for us at around 5am while we were on our way to Wallington. We were eventually cornered for a second time when Joe drove into a cul-de-sac after being rammed in the back by a police car. Joe was caught after falling through a chicken-coop roof – he eventually served nine months.

Our gang even had night watchmen on the take; of course, this beats ramraiding, but the risks are still as great, as one night we were slightly pissed and had left a car loaded with hoisty gear when a copper spotted a door open. Someone came to our party and told us, so we had to get rid of the car sharpish. One copper was left standing under an arch nearby while his pal went for reinforcements. We jumped in and drove off – with the copper on the bonnet smashing away at the windscreen with his truncheon! We soon shook him off.

We'd use scaffolding batons from building sites and put them against a shop front, reverse the car up to the baton and wallop, in the shop front would go and it didn't make too much noise. That's how it was and, apart from the use of updated vehicles, nothing much has changed except they now just blatantly reverse the vehicle through the shutters, or just drive straight through plate-glass doors.

Just like when I was young they're game for anything, this new breed of ramraider, even pulling out cash machines with hydraulic lifting arms mounted on wagons – cheeky lot. Just lucky them cash machines weren't around when I was active otherwise we'd have had the lot of them.

The term 'ramraider' has been glamorised by the press and the media; there was even a film made called *Shopping*, which I believe was banned in certain parts of the country – now here's the book.

I leave you with some words from my book *Respect*:

'Chaps, an almost mythical grouping of criminals whose ethos includes: professionalism in the pursuit of crime; loyalty to others of their kind; hatred of any co-operation with authority, and courage. Many aspire to membership, few qualify.'

RESPECT – *Freddie Foreman*

INTRODUCTION

AS YOU'VE READ in the Foreword, Freddie Foreman got up to some pretty powerful stuff in his time: he's been there – the book, the T-shirt and more. What is within this book is very much akin to what Freddie got up to in his early years, and he followed through to become an icon. The characters portrayed in this book have not emulated Freddie, with the exception of a guy called Faggo (as in having a 'fag' with a 'go' on the end), who was the most skilled motor-vehicle driver ever to have set foot on the ramraid circuit. His motorbike prowess is legendary within the circles he mixed in. Faggo, though, didn't follow it through, but I believe he could have, in a different environment.

The crimes within this book are all about motor-vehicle-related crimes. A modern-day tool is the computer, not that I know much about the workings within it, although I know how to use one, so it is with the ramraiders – they sure could use a powerful motor.

The blame for the ramraiding craze throughout the world can be squarely laid at the door of the north-east of England. Exported to the four corners of the world like a tormented beast gone crazy with a rage on wheels. Others consider that the north-east was only capable of exporting coal, but here was a new phenomenon being unleashed. Just like the people that keep perpetuating the story that the north of England is full of whippet breeders wearing flat caps, it is similarly no use trying to escape the plaudits and accolades from within the crime underworld that are thrown to the modern-day anti-heroes within – artists of their short-lived profession.

Many worse things have come out of the north of England; Catherine Cookson has perpetuated the north's long-suffering fight against inequality. Books full of nostalgic dribble about flat-capped, hard-done-to northerners – the world just fucking loves it and here are all of us northerners being looked on as some dark-age cult with a language all of our own, when all what we want to do is break free. That's all these ramraiders wanted to do – break free from themselves.

They wanted to break the chain of constant poverty and shower their loved ones with gifts of new clothing, furniture and other ill-gotten gains that might help them change their lives. Catherine Cookson was from a bygone age that seemed nostalgic, but really the poor fuckers were dying from all sorts of poverty-related disease. Now that the north has been connected to the National Grid there are all sorts of electrical gadgets available to us and, of course, we can all sit and watch Catherine Cookson repeats and *Byker Grove* while we eat our mushy peas and black pudding from our à la carte menu.

For those of you who are not yet familiar with my style of writing, I must point out that I stretch the word grammar to as tight a punctuation as it will go – meaning I don't give a toss about it. That's not out of any disrespect or some hidden malfunction within me, but out of respect to you all. After all, this book isn't likely to be read by a university professor of the English language. How do I know that? Because I get plenty of feedback from you guys and gals out there, some in prisons with bars and some in prisons of their own making. I've only ever had one person say that the punctuation was shite and that person was from another planet as far as being able to communicate with my loyal following.

I believe in something called 'Live Writing', you should try it; you write something down and then no matter what, you have to leave it as it is! What says you academics do that, it's nothing new as it first originated in the States. I've simply taken that idea and tweaked it up a bit. No different to ramraiding really, you make the decision and go for it; last one to jump in is a tosser! We've bastardised the English language, taken it and beaten it to a pulp, and now you can get to grips with something readable.

I have been accused, though, of writing in such a way that I don't credit my readers with any intelligence! I don't like that accusation because I've always credited my readers with an intelligence that sets them apart from the usual run-of-the-mill punter who would rather sit watching *Byker Grove,* week after week. If the police had shown that to the ramraiders when questioning them it would have made them talk thirty to the dozen.

We need a real drama series. I mean, all people ever do when they visit the north is make films in old castles while trying to make with an Americanised Scottish accent, then we go and pay a fortune to watch our own castles on the big screen all the way back over from Gloucester to the Arran isles, as that is what I class as northern England. So you lot living south of Gloucester haven't got much turf to play on; mind you, I've a lot of pals down souf so I can't really wallop their part of the kingdom too much as they don't arf give me a warm welcome when I visit – easy with the shandy, lads.

This book is going to take us places; you can imagine yourself to be one of the villains, feel the tension build up, feel the power surge of the turbo engine, hear the squeal of the wheels, the roar of the engine and later on … the slap of the cuffs as they go on!

While reading this you're probably sitting on a worn-out settee or in the corner of a prison cell, or in a warmer climate while holidaying abroad, hiding from the police more than likely. I doubt very much if you're gonna be sitting on a seven-grand three-piece while being fed grapes, although I do know a few that might fit that bill. So it is out of respect for you that I write in my own inimitable style.

The opening section on ramraids is just a taster that I've nicked from various newspaper cuttings and public knowledge. I mean, I'd be lying if I said it was all hard graft in collating this one and that one.

The section after that goes into it better and therefore it could be classed as a double-edged book in what it gives you. First a narrative of associated crimes and then the heavy stuff. I can tell you that the fear and concern given off by one of the actual ramraiders made them withdraw from helping with this book. The fear and concern wasn't a fear of physical violence, but it was a fear of being recharged with offences.

I can tell you, though, that one ramraider and a mystery man did come forward to set the record straight. What is within here is for the history books so we may as well try to get it right; thanks to Faggo & Co we achieve this.

I have employed researchers, which I allow myself the luxury of, as I've sat around too many reference libraries in my time. I was once accused (and laughed at mockingly) about a book that I used six researchers for; the laugh was one of those fake ones, as if to say, 'You lying bastard, you didn't employ six researchers on that, you're taking the piss.' What would your reaction have been, send the boys round and have them sorted or what? I knew my talents were wasted on them and that they'd never be in our league. Me and you, the reader, are in our own circle and I'd gladly spend time with you sharing a pint or a whisky, as we don't need such egg heads to share our time.

I'm not in the game of mugging anyone off or knocking them down a peg when they haven't done anything to deserve it, and with that I thank you for taking the time to listen to my ramblings. For those loyal readers who've waited patiently for this book, may I thank you for being so loyal and going out and buying it, borrowing or managing just to obtain it somehow, as I have heard that crime books are the most lucrative books for shoplifters to go out and nick, naughty, naughty. I know none of my loyal followers would go out and do that, would you, so keep the faith.

Max Respect, Stay Strong
Stephen Richards, 2005

CHAPTER ONE

PRACTICE MAKES PERFECT

HERE WE ARE in a new millennium and yet the legacy of past ramraids is still with us. Broken businesses, broken dreams and shattered hopes lie in the mangled wreckage of thousands of staved-in shop fronts, the perpetrators of such crimes having shed their overactive desire to shop for goods with stolen vehicles by driving them through steel shutters and plate-glass windows – or at least having their desires castrated by the severe penalties dished out to particular gangs held up as examples for all to take heed of.

When ramraids were thwarted by the ingenuity or luck of those being victimised, there were plenty more retail outlets to rape and strip of their goods. This chapter acts as a reminder, an '*aide memoir*', to build up to the ending, which revolves around a specific gang that danced with death on many an occasion. They gambled with their raw talents, they were Eddie Kidd and Evel Knievel mixed into one, they gave entertainment value for the public, fed to them via the media. But, like all things, fashions change, and like anything else this once in-vogue element will make a comeback. In the meantime let's take a look back over the time when this phenomenon took the north-east region of England, then the rest of the UK and finally the world, by storm.

I could be accused of glamorising crime, the favourite question on all journalists' lips whenever they ask about anyone writing about such things. The answer to that must be an emphatic 'Yes'. We've come to expect our icons of the criminal world to be larger than life, better than anyone else at foiling the final capture scene. We all love a good thriller, so here it is for real.

How often we've willed Steve McQueen to be able to jump his stolen motorbike over that barbed-wire fence in the film *The Great Escape*, even though we've seen the act fail time after time. We still want him to escape. *The Italian Job*: didn't we want to see them get away with it? Of course. Remember the end of the film when one of the characters says, 'Hold on, I've got an idea.' What the fuck was the idea? Didn't we want the film to go on a little longer? I sure did. What of those other films that have become part of our repeat-TV diet? We know the ending but we always hope, and that's why we've come to champion the cause of the underdog.

Don't forget that most of those carrying out these ramraids were doing so out of necessity and, of course, 'necessity' is, as we know, 'the mother of invention'. 'Necessity', though, eventually turned into greed. More wasn't enough. Daring became a challenge to the ramraiders in outrunning the authorities, who only had a real break when the gang were all grassed up. Good policing or detective work had nothing to do with the capture of the main gang, but more of that in the relevant chapter – let's crack on.

April 1987 – 'Try and try again' was the motto in use by these gangs. A bungled raid on a clothes shop in the West End of Newcastle didn't put off the occupants of a stolen turbo-powered Saab. The clothes shop was rammed to such a degree that it caused masonry to fall on to the vehicle. There was nothing else for it but to travel at high speed across Newcastle to nearby Jesmond, home to the hoity-toity brigade – yeah, there's sure to be one of them posh wine stores there, what's it called, '*Winterschladen*'?

The rear doors to the off-licence were rammed and the load-up of fags was fast – supersonic fast: some £1,500 worth was taken. Invariably the damage caused was far more in excess of the value of goods stolen and that was the case in both of these raids.

Finding the right 'G' spot was going to take some practice to hone the skills needed for future raids.

Although residents were awakened by noise from the raid on the off-licence and they witnessed the booty being loaded up, they made no attempt to stop the crime. Ordinarily, such a crime would be bound to attract some sort of Rambo character out of his mud hut, but this was a crime against unseen victims – commercial victims.

OK, we all know that commercial insurance premiums are hiked up due to this sort of thing; repairs to premises after such raids would make many business a high risk. Who'd risk their lives to stop such a commercial robbery? Not many! We'd nearly all protect our neighbours from such an attack because we know them, but people that we don't know, who run most business ventures, have to fight their own battles.

This off-licence had been victim to umpteen previous robberies; now the upgraded version was to hit them.

May 1987 – Driving skills were going to have to be improved on – this raid proves it. This was the second raid on one of Tyneside's home electrical suppliers. Luxury goods were targeted – video recorders. OK, we've nearly all got one of these contraptions, now outdated by DVD, but back then these machines were bringing £100 to £150 from the right people and there were plenty of people willing to forgo the usual one- to three-year warranty in order to save a few hundred quid.

A stolen van from the renamed 'Water Board' was used to ram the shop window. The goods were loaded into another stolen vehicle, this time a turbo-powered Metro. Oh yes, they needed the kudos of a high-powered car and if it was black it made it even better to sport around town in. The car was spotted by British Rail Transport Police, last seen by them powering its way out of Newcastle city centre at a fast rate of knots.

In hot pursuit was a police vehicle that gave the occupants of the stolen Metro a sufficient enough fright to make the driver lose control and bend the metal. The four occupants scampered out of sight into a rambling housing estate of rat runs and the police soon gave up the chase – the stolen video recorders were left behind.

This was the second strike on these retail premises within weeks and it's proven that lightning does strike twice at the same place. If you've been unlucky enough to be burgled, then the fact is you're more than likely to be targeted for a second try, and so it was to be the case here. Believing that they wouldn't dare come back has been disproved; back then it wasn't as common knowledge as it is now, although there are many that still fall for the three-card trick that they'll not come back.

Many people weren't too concerned about such raids as, after all, it wasn't like they were targeting domestic premises, and some of the ramraiders actually prided themselves that they wouldn't touch a domestic dwelling.

August 1987 – Proving once again that lightning can strike twice at the same place, and that the ramraiders were a little bit ahead of the psychologists, they struck for a second time at a fashion store – making an entrance as usual. They rammed through the glass doors only a week after their first raid on the Benetton store, in Newcastle upon Tyne. The previously rammed glass doors were, rather stupidly, replaced with new glass doors for the ramraiders to re-enact their previous ploy. This time they used a stolen Ford Fiesta to do their bidding.

Police were completely unaware and taken by total surprise in this raid, in which some £4,000 worth of clothes were stolen, mainly to order, as the ramraiders would gather intelligence about their target. When the raid took place, the job went with military precision. All the items would be spoken for, even to be worn by some of the gang members in their next raid ... well, they had to maintain their image of being slaves to fashion – and they did it with style.

A spokesman for the shop went on to say how they didn't think this would happen again after the last raid – hmmm! Things were only just warming up.

The ramraiders had some cheek in returning to the store for a further raid. This double hit made the staff wonder whether they were coming or going. A raid takes place at 2.30am on Sunday, the shop is boarded up and a few hours later, at 5.30am, the gang strike again, this time with a stolen Ford Granada taking £3,000 worth of clothing but causing some £10,000 worth of damage!

The city centre is policed by a local police station, yet the raiders were able to put a thumb up to their nose and wiggle their fingers at the police – this was only the beginning.

August 1987 – A gang of robbers pulled off a £¾ million heist, the biggest job pulled off in the north-east of England (further details in Viv (Graham) – *Simply the Best*). This was a ramraid and a robbery combined. A top-of-the-range Range Rover was stolen from a Newcastle showroom. The sturdy metal gates of the loading bay of the main Sorting Office, in West Sunniside, Sunderland were going to take some opening; the Range Rover was the perfect tool. Up to six stolen vehicles were used in this 'Ramborry'.

There were two men in the Range Rover when it cracked open the gates. The gates had just been locked after a van loaded with dosh arrived from Newcastle. The van was unloaded and the money was put on to a trolley, and as if by magic the robbers seemed to know just when to strike. In went the gates and a gang of men armed with weapons ranging from shotguns to pickaxe handles determined that the cash was going to be theirs, one way or another. All went well and the cash was loaded into a waiting Ford Transit van. I have it on good authority that this raid nearly didn't result in a score for the men; one of them hesitated and nearly turned back. Maybe I can elaborate further in *Viv and the Geordie Mafia Vol. III*.

At a later date, two men were to be targeted for allegedly having played a role in this ramborry. Both men claimed to have alibis and a subsequently lengthy trial followed. The name of one of the men charged with the robbery was John H Sayers; he was to be acquitted.

John H Sayers was to receive a 15-year custodial sentence in February 1990 for a serious offence he had been charged with in November 1989. Sayers is now a free man after having served his sentence.

September 1987 – A hat-trick of ramraids was to take place in the same day. Records were starting to be broken.

Crash! In goes the British Home Stores window in the now common tradition – driving a car through it. This time a Ford Capri was used in this daring raid in the prestigious Northumberland Street of Newcastle. Did these ramraiders have no respect for such a street lined with dignified household High Street chain stores? Of course not. Some nice clothes would come in handy.

Bang! Another Ford, this time a Granada, is used to smash through the exterior of Curry's electrical shop. OK, it was a few miles away up the old Spine Road, in the forlorn pit town of Ashington. Newcastle/Ashington, so what! So long as the places had shops to raid nothing was going to be safe from this lot. They stole a food mixer! Not quite the FST TV they had in mind, eh? Oh well, practice makes perfect and these lads were still learning the ropes. Their raw and rusty methods left a lot to be desired but they had a talent, that's for sure.

Wallop! – The Ford Granada hasn't quite been finished with yet. There's life in it so it's used to strike at the town's social club. Not satisfied with a food mixer they decide to drive at the doors of the club, but not enough power – or was it bottle? – is applied. The Granada was certainly left for dead after that little lot.

October 1987 – Another Ford car is used to ram shop-front shutters. Blayney's off-licence was the ideal target for the ramraiders, but the car wasn't powerful enough to dislocate the shutters from their mountings. Even though the force was enough to send a shock wave that moved a freezer some 20 feet inside the shop, the shutters remained solidly in place. The skill of using an alternative, more powerful vehicle to do the actual ramming still had to be learned.

October 1987 – To give you some idea of the desperation to line pockets with silver because of low wages and the poverty trap, here's a short story that might help you to understand the desperate measures men will stoop to when in need. Some amongst the security guards employed to watch over the giant food cash and carry of Batley's in Durham ended up breaking into it on a regular basis. £63,000 was the estimated value put on goods to have been stolen over a period of three months by the gang of guards. They were employed to keep a watchful eye over the premises, but greed got the better of them and it was common knowledge among the guards that this was going on. It ended up with some of them being jailed; there's no need to embarrass the men by naming them. It goes to show that if these sort of people, who were meant to be protecting such sites, turn into vultures then what chance would unemployed young men have to resist such urges; those setting the example were no longer angels or paragons of virtue, so what chance would these little council-estate cherubs stand in being able to resist the attraction of deluxe quality goods? None.

October 1987 – Yet another Ford car was used in a ramraid, this time a Sierra. Newcastle, again, was the favourite haunt – another quality clothing shop. Burton's menswear in Blackett Street was the target; a successful raid saw the spoils of war carried off. The shop, plundered and pillaged, was left in a state of demolition.

This time the police happened by and gave chase. The car, with contents, was dumped some miles away, complete with its cargo of branded goods. 'Hello, hello, hello, what 'ave we 'ere then?' The goods were successfully returned, but the raiders had escaped to be able to ram another day.

October 1987 – Remember when anyone who was anyone, or anyone who wanted to be someone, would wear leather? Well, it looked like a lot of people would be wearing leather after this ramraid. Remember those tacky-coloured leathers – red, blue, green, mixed colours and even some with tassels, so when you lifted your arms up the tassels made you look like the Angel of the North (yuk!)? Boy, you were the hardest bastard on the block if you had one of these and a Honda 50 to match.

£8,000 worth of leathers was stolen in this better-organised raid; they were starting to get their act together. This raid would have ten operatives; the site security guard was blocked in his caravan when a car reversed up against the door. One of the raiders smashed the window, shouting all sorts of threats that the guard wouldn't see the light of day if he made a silly move – he stayed put.

Another car was used to reverse into the door of this aptly named retailer, Leather Factory, on an industrial estate in North Tyneside. With over 160 leathers at, say, 'Fifty quid to you, guv,' it was quite a nice little earner that would see eight grand being added to the local underworld economy – until the unemployment giro arrived, that is. This was the second raid on the Leather Factory. The first was staged in the first week of its opening – these guys were quick to spot a bargain.

October 1987 – 'Lightning never strikes at the same place twice', so they say. Ramraiders, though, can strike at the same place four times. That old favourite of theirs was the 'Benetton' store in Newcastle's Grey Street. This was a ramraid done on the cheap. A metal bin was used to smash through the window, although a car was used to cart off the prestigious brand-name goods.

The manager of the shop was convinced that the goods were being taken away and sold on the Continent. Had anyone bothered to take a look around over the next few days, they would have been surprised to see how many youngsters in and around Newcastle were sporting new 'Benetton' clothes. This craze for obtaining clothes from Benetton shops continued throughout the country. Word had obviously spread that these were the clothes to be seen in. £17,000 worth of clothing wouldn't have taken up much room; after all, how many carrier bags of fashionable clothing can you get for, say, a grand?

If you ever want to get into management then take note of how bright you have to be. The Area

Manager commented to someone that 'There must be a ready market for our stock.' As bright as a dud sparkplug, eh?

October 1987 – Across the Tyne, in Gateshead's Ellison Street, another Ford car was being put through its paces to see if it could withstand a collision with a metal shutter. The shutter came off worse when the Granada pounded its way into the television showroom of DER. Back then, a video could be used to buy your way into any self-respecting person's confidence.

Three vids were valued at a grand each. Of course, it had only taken about ten grand's worth of damage to get them. A couple of hundred quid for each of them, though, would bring smiles of joy to the faces of the buyers at getting such a bargain. Compare that to the current price vids go for – depreciation is shocking!

October 1987 – OK, fashions change and now nobody would be seen dead wearing leather, not since those Berghaus jackets and fancy wax jacket things were starting to be worth a few bob more than ordinary leather. Brand names were much nicer for the counterfeiters to copy; I mean, what's the use of counterfeiting leather? But that's not going to be covered here, so on with the story.

The Berghaus factory in Washington, the north-east's answer to Milton Keynes, was rammed with – guess what? – a Ford Escort. When security men found the car embedded into the building, its engine was still running. The raid was a little more unusual in that it happened in the late evening. Goods robbed included Gortex outdoor clothing and other specialised outdoor clothing – it can get very cold in the north-east of England. £14,000 worth of clothing had gone for a burton, to pardon a pun.

We can see the art form starting to show through now. The earlier raids were rather clumsy, albeit practical, and items of less value were targeted; now anyone could afford a Berghaus jacket. The man from Del Monte, he say 'Yes'.

March 1988 – Just a reminder that the Ford Capri has got some sort of use after all. A trader was travelling with his takings to a bank, in Hebburn, near to Jarrow, Tyneside. The raiders were obviously armed with inside information from what is known in the trade as a 'card marker'. Their card was marked that he was carrying cash and they devised a plan in which the Ford Capri would be driving in front of the trader's van, a humble Sherpa, and would stop suddenly and reverse into the front of the van. The simple plan worked and three masked men leaped out of some bushes on the roadside.

What was likely to go wrong did go wrong. Police had described the raid as 'carefully planned'. What, though, could the trader do now? While you're thinking about that, I'll tell you that one of the windows was smashed on the van; this tactic is often carried out to disturb the victim. Banging and other sounds can be more frightening to someone who isn't used to this sort of thing than actual applied violence – called 'understating'.

This 'carefully planned' raid, however, was botched; the trader simply put his van into reverse gear and drove away – happily unscathed and a lot wiser for it. Freddie Foreman, our Foreword writer, would have had the vehicle blocked in from all angles; for those of you who have seen film footage of one of his raids, you'll know what I mean. The difference there, though, was that one of the two armed security guards in the van, which was carrying an awful lot more than a trader's takings, shot and killed one of the gang Freddie was with. None of the gang was armed with a gun. That was the start of 'gun law'.

Getting back to this rather more humble raid, the desperate measures applied by this gang in order to get a few pounds in cash of an honest man's takings was disproportionate to what a ramraid gang would be sharing out among themselves, and with far less risk of a large prison sentence. This sort of raid could carry a five- or seven-year prison sentence, depending on what previous form the men had. Compare that to a ramraid. What could you expect in terms of a prison sentence for one ramraid?

May 1988 – That old favourite carriage of the ramraiders, the Ford Granada, was being used for what it seems best designed for – ramming into steel. They say that about 5 per cent of police arrests happen because the police just happen to be near to the scene of a crime. Opportunists, you might say. That's what happened here. Unbeknown to the ramraiders, parked up in the same street as them, in North Shields, was an occupied police car.

As was usual, a second car was waiting for the booty to be loaded into it, but on this occasion the ciggies and booze had to be left when the police arrived on the scene – the raiders escaped.

May 1988 – This next raid is for the connoisseurs among you. Ramraiding is, I believe, an art form. Just as some lunatics go to some far-flung gallery to look at some other lunatic sleeping in a bed, and being paid for it as well, I believe this should be preserved as a piece of social history. I mean, when you think of how gullible people are, it makes sense. What about the man that sold Tower Bridge, in London, to an American? What about the fools from a gallery who paid good money for a pile of bricks? And what about those body parts in jars put on display? Am I making more sense than those people? I hope so.

Durham city had just opened the doors to the newly built showpiece Milburngate Shopping Complex. Most cities were developing this style of complex at the time, so why shouldn't Durham have one too? The complex was a magnate for shoppers and scouts? Scouts, yes, scouts. You know, the ones that go on ahead looking for items of interest and all that? Well, this was no different. Scouts from the gang would go and look over the site for any potential flaws or weaknesses that would allow them to ramraid. A 'recky', reconnaissance – a spying mission. These ramraiders were certainly coming up in the world.

Dixon's electrical store was to be the target. Full of merchandise that would line their empty pockets, there was going to be one hell of a party after all the stuff was sold on through their eagerly awaiting crowd of bulk buyers. Security guards meant nothing to these raiders. After all, no one was likely to risk his or her life for the rewards of a small pay packet at the end of the week. 'Stand and deliver.'

The glass entry doors would be a doddle. A flick of the wrist on the steering wheel and around she would go, up the mall – that hundred yards would be easy – and then line the baby up, 'cos she was gong straight through that motherfucker of a window. TRANGHHHHHH! 'Fucking hell, back it up, try again.' 'Fuck me, what's it made of, fucking steel?' Triple laminated glass seemed to be rather difficult to drive through; they had to make a sharp exit.

This raid, though, was possibly the start of bigger things and has to be considered an ideal training run for further raids on such monstrously carbuncle-shaped complexes. The fact that the building was invaded caused some embarrassment for the centre management. God, was nothing safe from these raiders? The bottle it must have taken to do such a raid is unimaginable. There you are, revving the balls off the car, into gear it goes, the foot comes off the clutch and you're heading for plate-glass doors. What if some of the glass comes through the windscreen, what if …?

'No time for such thoughts, you just have to fucking get on with it,' I was told from one retired ramraider. 'You don't bottle out, you've got no time to drop your arse and you haven't just got yourself to think about. What gives you the drive is knowing that within two or three minutes you're gonna have what you want.'

We've all seen the SAS storming of the Iraqi embassy. You know, the one in which half a dozen masked SAS guys swing down on ropes and fly through the embassy windows while smoke pisses out. That sort of thing stood this country in good stead; it was a good shop window to display the goods to the rest of the world, like saying, 'Fuck with us and that's what you get.' OK, ramraiders aren't going in to face real bullets, although Freddie Foreman and his men did and as previously mentioned one died because of it. But the actual spirit of true grit it takes to carry out such a ramraid shows what these guys were made of.

These guys weren't going out to mug old women or

to burgle dwelling houses, nothing so low for them. It doesn't mean that the crime was or is acceptable, but it was far superior and more acceptable than rape, murder or robbery and the likes. If we had the choice of living next door to a ramraider or next door to a dwelling-house burglar, we all know the choice we'd rather take. I know that some among you will argue the case for not living next door to any type of criminal, in the perfect world.

July 1988 – Not exactly a ramraid, but a sensational getaway in a car more at home running up and down the Boulevard in Monte Carlo than downtown Gateshead. A stolen Porsche with a very distinctive private registration plate was used in a raid on the equally up-market off-licence *Winterschladen*, in Newcastle's penthouse area of Jesmond – what better car to use? A very classy raid. A haul of ciggies and booze was going to be making its way across the foggy River Tyne, over the sodium-lit Tyne Bridge – in the wrong lane, of course.

The car was eventually to be dumped in the area of Felling, Gateshead. The two-man gang was going to be mourning the loss of their booty as they fled on foot. The car chase had seen the Porsche ram a police car and drive at break-neck speed into a housing estate. The art of good raiding was to ensure your getaway would avoid such areas; any good ramraider wouldn't want to get charged with death by reckless driving. Not that this was a ramraid to use as an example for others to follow. But similar raids were thought to have been carried out by the same gang. The thought of being caught seemed to have given them a total disregard for the safety of the public – naughty!

November 1988 – Compare this type of ramraid to the one previously mentioned and it will be obvious to you what the difference is between an art form and total abandonment of sanity. The infamous Studio nightclub in Newcastle was the scene for mayhem and madness. The club was later to be the setting for the murder of Penny Laing, glassed in her throat by a man she rebutted for touching her up. Another pointless murder in the centre of Newcastle; the list of those that have been attacked, stabbed, slashed and murdered is endless.

This time, the cursed nightclub was to be the target of a ramraider. A witness in the club was able to recount what happened. 'I was standing with a group of friends and the sound of wood being cut by a chainsaw could be heard in the distance. I thought it was a bit odd, as we were in a nightclub in the centre of Newcastle, not Kielder Forest. The fire doors behind us burst open and this car shot through them with an almighty fucking crash. If it weren't so serious I would have thought it was that paedophile Gary Glitter coming in on one of his big choppers he used to ride on to stage with years ago. This "old bloke" threw a flare, or what I thought was a flare, into the place. The 'old bloke' was actually an old bloke face mask, so the person could have been any age. All I know after that is that we were surrounded by smoke coming from this flare thing that was chucked in. By the time we got to the door the geezer had fucked off. If he had still been there he would have been pulled to pieces by the crowd – spoiled a fucking good night out that did.'

When you consider the seriousness of the attack, and that the police station was just around the corner, it shows the lack of brains the ramraider had. No monetary gain, just revenge, as this was the only obvious motive. A crowd of nightclubbers could have been so easily killed in the rush to escape the fumes and smoke. What if anyone had been leaning against the inside of the fire door? This sort of attack would have probably led to a life sentence and still will if the attacker/s is/are ever caught or grassed up for the offence. Some lout with a grudge willing to kill, all over what? That sort of raid couldn't be classed as art.

January 1989 – Moving on from the previous raid, we now see one of the best cars for the job being used; in fact, Renault might have been accused of designing this shopping trolley on wheels with the ramraider in mind. The Renault 5 Turbo was an ideal vehicle for this sort of crime. Fast, very fast … nippy, a neat little hatch to help a speedy load-up and a nice wide-opening door to be able to jump into or out of – Armani couldn't have done better.

Matthews Sports in Whitley Bay was the target of an early-morning raid. Gone was the bulkier Ford Granada. Two agile and nimble Renault 5 Turbo cars were used – last seen blazing a trail towards North Shields.

June 1989 – One of the ultimate cars at that time to be used in a ramraid was the now classic Ford Sierra Cosworth Flip, capable of outrunning most things – 500bhp. At the time it was the obvious choice, as well as a status symbol to be seen in – only the best ramraiders would be seen in these cars. Gone was the basic Mondeo or Escort ... I mean, what self-respecting ramraider wanted to be caught in a Mondeo?

The tools of the trade were becoming obvious: a Ford pickup was used to ram the steel shutters while two Cosworths waited nearby to the Victoria Wine Store in Jarrow. By now the risk of being caught was as slim as a Rizla paper. There was more chance of being caught taking a piss in a side street than for doing a ramraid – or so this gang thought. Wrong! The police had been tipped off and lay in wait.

The gang of eight were masked up, as the risk of being caught was now thought to be from CCTV. They weren't taking any chances and, just to look a little bit sinister, they carried baseball bats. Dave

Courtney, a retired London underworld figure, once said, 'What's the point of anyone carrying a serious weapon, say, a gun or a knife? What if the gun's imitation and you come to point it at someone? You can't use it, but you're gonna get serious time. What if you use the knife or threaten to use it? That's why I used to carry my knuckle-duster. I'd use it. It gave me a chance. Them carrying the other types of weapon would be standing there not knowing what the fuck to do. The difference was that I'd not be facing quarter the time they'd be facing from the courts.'

So in a way, if we look at it from DC's point of view, they were cutting down the chances of killing someone, but they could still look mean and if need be they would use them to make good their escape. As it happens, the police caught two of the gang at the scene and no one was injured. The rest of the gang made their getaway down the A1. The police were left behind as the powerful Cosworths disappeared into the moonlight, and later; one was to be found miles away. They'd got away to ramraid another day, as surely they would. All of the vehicles were stolen and maybe this is why the insurance premium for a Ford Sierra Cosworth was often more than the value of the car!

June 1989 – In keeping with the style of car now acceptable to ramraid gangs, a VW Golf GTi was used in a very useless raid on a tenanted pub on Gateshead's Chowdene Bank, called, at that time,

'Porcupine Park', now renamed 'The Gold Medal'. This gang was either extremely brave or extremely stupid. CRASHHHHH! In went the double front doors, rammed with a car. An inner set of double doors was also demolished, all for the sake of the contents from a few gaming machines. The courts would have imposed a very, very severe custodial sentence on this gang if they were caught.

Someone in the building at the time confronted the gang. On hearing the noise, he reached for a golf club – luckily for the gang, as I've heard of some publicans keeping loaded guns for such cases! The ramraid could have turned nasty and into an aggravated burglary, which carries a pretty hefty sentence. The gang made a run for it and was chased by the club-wielding man. The club ended up being thrown through the rear window of one of their cars. Hope it wasn't an expensive club?

A pretty useless raid that was poorly planned and with little thought for the consequences. The gang returned to their old hunting ground of Jarrow – Fourbouy's Newsagency was their target. Ramraiding wasn't the same as robbing someone; if that was the case, they may as well have gone armed with a sawn-off and just pointed the gun – no, this was different. The gangs involved in this sort of crime weren't orientated towards heavy stuff, although a few of the rogue element gave it a try. This sort of crime was invented by a new breed of criminal. Bulk and muscle was a hindrance – agility was now in.

Endurance Man had arrived; speed, agility, quick succinct thinking and fast reflexes were required. A ramraider at his peak wouldn't need speed (amphetamines) to get a high; it was created from within. These gangs were the human equivalent of the Stealth Bomber, maybe even better – an Exocet.

July 1989 – A series of ramraids by the same gang in one night gave a small return. In the hope of securing some heavy returns from one raid that was a failure at Gateshead's Kwiksave Store, on the High Street, the gang desperately went on a spree that ended in a high-speed chase.

From the Kwiksave raid at Gateshead, the masked gang travelled in their stolen Ford Sierra Cosworth to Houghton-le-Spring, some eight or so miles away. The gang was spotted near to the Gateway superstore and fled empty handed after being spotted by the police. Things weren't going well at all.

Next was the Reg Vardy petrol kiosk at Houghton-le-Spring, too tough to get into so they gave up and ended up travelling at speeds in excess of 100mph back towards Gateshead. This gang was travelling around in circles and spoiling for a decent haul, and try, try and try again they did. It all ended in nothing and this night out was going to really piss off both the police and the ramraiders with a final dig at the

Gateway Store, in Gateshead's prestigious showcase Metro Centre. They'd all live to raid another day.

September 1990 – Remember what Dave Courtney said about carrying weapons? North Shields, North Tyneside was the familiar setting for another ramraid, this time on an independent trader's shop. A dark back alley was the scene of this failed and very idiotic ramraid. A gang of five masked men were getting it on and in the process of gaining entry to the premises in the normal way – ramming the double doors with a car. Only one problem though. A local man was nearby. He was just leaving a takeaway when he noticed the alarm box flashing at the rear of his father's shop.

He didn't hesitate in seeking out what was wrong – he soon found out and was lucky to come away with his life! Visible in the lane was a Vauxhall Astra reversing at speed into the double back doors, and also prominent was a masked man holding a handgun. 'Don't come any closer or I'll blow your fucking head off,' the masked man shouted as he pointed the gun towards the man. The Astra was now reversing at some speed towards the back doors of the shop, smashing them off their hinges. The man acted without concern for his own safety when he stood his ground, goading the raiders. A second car, which the ramraiders had all jumped into, was driven at him and as he dived for safety, the car came at him again. The man ran for cover, leaving the raiders to make their getaway empty handed.

This sort of raid wasn't carried out by true blue-blooded ramraiders. A handgun, use of the car as a weapon and very basic use of their acumen indicated that this was a counterfeit gang masquerading as ramraiders.

Any ramraider worth their salt would have thought this out, and the use of such violent actions could have led to a young man's death. If caught, the gang would have all faced life imprisonment. Carrying such a weapon would put the user in such a position that he or she would have known that to use it could have resulted in a death. Sorry to have to put it so basically. I do credit you, my reader, with intelligence but I want to be absolutely sure that the point is hammered home. Supposing you answered the front door with a bread knife in your hand. You'd just been cutting bread and the person you opened the front door to attacked you. You defended yourself and in the process of doing so, the knife entered your attacker's heart – they died as a result of knife wounds. What would happen to you? Have a think about that one in terms of what the courts would probably say.

Now look at this example: the door bell rings, you look out of the window, see a stranger and purposefully go to the kitchen drawer, take out a bread knife and answer the door with it in your hand.

A fight follows and the man at your door dies from stab wounds. Compare that to the first example. The first example compared to this one can be compared to the ramraid scenario. One of the ramraiders purposefully carried a handgun. The mere fact that he didn't fire it doesn't matter one iota. The fact is that the innocent man involved in this ramraid thought he was going to be shot and that would have been sufficient for any judge, with half a brain, to proffer a fucking big prison sentence.

That's why any intelligent ramraider wouldn't have put themselves up for such a little reward in such a big way; after all, this was only a shop being turned over, not Fort fucking Knox.

October 1990 – Washington New Town, as it was once called, has now become plain 'Washington'. Designed by an architect that seems to have based the design of this area on the principles of the children's game 'Blind Man's Bluff', this was the ideal place with its rat runs and long, clean-cut roads for high-performance Cosworth-type cars to be used by opportunist burglars.

The ramraiders had paved the way in showing others that high-powered cars were ideal for carrying stolen goods from A to B – simple as that. So it was obvious that other crime factions would follow suit and utilise the idea in other types of crime – like burglary.

The basic principle of knocking on the doors of

dimly lit houses without alarms applied to small gangs in their twenties seeking out the spoils that would help buy them their next fix or drink. Knock! Knock! No answer. The door would be jemmied open and, within seconds, the contents of the living room were piled into a powerful getaway car. One raid netted them £6,500 worth of goods from the living room alone. Twenty seconds later, the car on standby would be off and within minutes it could be out of the area altogether. Ford Escort XR3i, Golf GTi, Mitsubishi Sports and a whole other bunch of head turners were used in such raids, all as a direct result of ramraiders setting the example.

November 1990 – LD Mountain Centre in Newcastle's Dean Street was a typical target at the time of year leading up to Christmas; after all, something special would be needed for little Jimmy's or little Jenny's present. Bollards or no bollards, this job was on.

A stolen gas van was the missile used to batter the steel shutters down. Expensive high-tech ski jackets were loaded into a waiting car and off they went, but this time an eagle-eyed traffic cop spotted the dodgy-looking crew and gave chase. The result: car is abandoned, the gang escape and goods are recovered. L & D Mountain Centre and other outlets were starting to get sick of the same seasonal happening. Was the worm about to turn?

November 1990 – £16,000 worth of DIY goods including power tools were stolen in a ramraid on the Texas Homecare store on the Silverlink Industrial Estate at Wallsend, the shipbuilding village, Newcastle. Fire-exit doors were rammed and hey presto – Aladdin's Cave!

December 1990 – The Makro food and clothing store on the Wear Industrial Estate at Washington was successfully rammed in a tasteful raid. A previous ramraid at the front of the building had resulted in bollards being planted in the ground, now that the horse had bolted; better bolt the door – not fucking likely!

Nice Christmas present for the ramraiders this, in the form of £20,000 worth of goods, but between about twenty of them it wouldn't last five minutes. A stolen car was used around the side of the building, which was bollard free. Although staff and security guards were working in the store, it didn't matter one iota to the gang. Only two hours previously the store had been open to the public. Some of the raiders were carrying pickaxe handles, although they were more for show than for actual use – some gangs actually did use them, and guns.

Security staff just stood back out of harm's way; after all, this wasn't like apprehending a lone shoplifter or two, the gang was en masse and armed at that – fuck that for a lark.

This sort of raid epitomises what it was all about – smooth. No heroics from members of the gang, nothing too flash in their weaponry and a quick in and out job.

December 1990 – Near to Christmas time this sort of raid was common, typified by a raid carried out on a chemists supply company on the formerly CCTV-free Team Valley Trading Estate, Gateshead. An Audi Quatro, no weakling of a car, was stolen for this ramraid on Darrela Supplies. The smelly stuff was in abundance in local pubs that year, even though the Audi broke down.

February 1991 – The Christmas pudding had not long settled and they were bang at it again. Up to now we've seen all sorts of high-performance cars and 4x4 vehicles used, all wonderful tools of the trade. These vehicles were sufficient to be able to do the job at hand, but at times the ramraiders would take a sledgehammer to crack a walnut, as is the case in the following raid.

A stolen JCB (named after the manufacturer – J C Bamford), which for those of you wondering is a large wheeled machine with a mechanical bucket at the front and a large mechanical arm at the rear, weighing in at a mean 7½ tons, was used to ram through the wall of an off-licence and tobacconist shop in Sydney Street, North Shields. A gang of six men then systematically looted ciggies and booze.

February 1991 – Masked ramraiders continued the post-Christmas rush by ramming a van into a supermarket (Nisa) at Allerdene, Gateshead.

February 1991 – Coxhoe in Durham didn't escape the February craze for ramraiding. An electrical store, Gatenby's, had its shutters rammed open and was stripped of electrical goods.

February 1991 – A jeweller's (now we were getting somewhere) was the target for the ramraid in North Shield's Bedford Street. In typical established manner, a vehicle was used to ram while another was on standby to make a quick, clean getaway – which it did.

March 1991 – Moving forward a little further in time and a little further afield to Teesside, we can see how the ramraid craze has spread to other areas.

Curry's electrical store on the South Bank Retail Park at Skipper's Lane was the target for this raid. A Ford Transit van was driven head-on through the security doors but only about £1,500 worth of goods were taken, in the form of a camcorder, Matsui TV set and a radio. Police cruising the area discovered the destruction left behind by the raiders.

Just looking at a few boring statistics, it was only a few months into 1991 and already there had been in excess of 30 ramraids in the Cleveland area. A sports shop in Redcar was ramraided by raiders repeatedly driving their car into the front of the building until entry was gained and a nice selection of clothes bundled away. Hyper UK suffered a £1,800 loss.

Billingham town centre didn't escape the wrath of the ramraid gods. A Mazda sports car smashed its way into Gentry Menswear; jeans and shirts totalling £2,500 were hauled away.

Owners of these outlets were now starting to press their hard-of-hearing councils for protection in the form of bollards being placed at the front of their premises. Not just yet though and basically only a visual deterrent!

May 1991 – When is too much, too much? Curry's and other multiples can carry certain losses, although that's not to say they should, but the small independent trader like Del 'boy' Trotter of Trotter's Independent Traders cannot suffer one loss, never mind two. This is what happened to 'Adonis' in Dundas Street, Redcar. Even though the premises had multiple locks on the door and meshed-up windows with an alarm system, it was no deterrent for determined resourceful ramraiders.

The second raid at this premises was to see £10,000 worth of stock go walkabout. Ramraiders, like judges, work without 'fear or favour' and this was the case here. The raid was over in minutes and the car used was an old favourite, the Astra GTE – a nice, neat, stolen, fast little car. The haul included some up-market Italian silk suits along with branded T-shirts and sweatshirts, which wouldn't be too hard to shift at the right price. Teesside's nightclubs were going to see some real bobby dazzlers turning up to show off their new togs.

August 1991 – Billingham is a rather unassuming place, sort of like a nondescript person. Not seen or heard, just there in the background, but then you start to notice characteristics and the once chameleon-like person can be given an identity to match what you see. That's what Billingham is like, quiet one minute and then the next minute, full of adventurous tourists seeking out the wonders of this hidden place.

Even though the annual international Folklore Festival was taking place, it didn't deter these ramraiders, for the second time in six weeks at Gentry's clothes shop. The raid took place at a time when tourists were walking about, in which some £2,000 worth of shell suits were yanked from the premises – will they ever come back into fashion? Remember those fucking horrible white ones? All I can say is don't go out in the snow with one on or you'll get knocked down by a snowplough!

October 1991 – Clothing shops were starting to become quite popular for ramraiders to target. You might be one of these people that see brand names as being your master, and if so you'll understand the addiction of wearing expensive designer labels. Ramraiders knew this sort of market existed and went for it: fashion slaves.

A stolen Astra van was driven into the doorway of Churchill's in Crescent Road, Harrogate. These ramraiders weren't seasoned professionals – the alarm went off and so did the raiders – like shit off a stick. Since two or more were involved in this you can imagine them saying, 'You ran first, so I ran.' 'No way, it was you, you ran first and I thought someone was coming.'

Seasoned professionals are going to be mentioned later on in this book. This is just the build-up, giving you the taste for the real thing. What about those readers of mine who read for escapism or pleasure? They like to have a build-up to things, so hang fire – don't hurry on just yet. We're going to be talking to Richard 'Faggo' Dodd, one of the lieutenants of the most successful ramraiding gang to come out of the north-east.

November 1991 – Riots had kicked off across the north-east (details in Viv (Graham) – *Simply the Best*). 'Booze' was the fuel needed to supply courage to the rioters, and what better way to go shopping than to ramraid. Ironically, the riots in Teesside had allegedly started after the arrest of a ramraider. This was mirrored on Tyneside earlier when two young men's lives ended in tragic circumstances during a police car chase. Two young men (Dale and Colin) were to be the reason that riots ignited on Tyneside, and on Teesside a similar scenario, but without the deaths, was being played out.

Former Northern Ireland soccer star, Eric McMordie, ran a supermarket on a Middlesbrough housing estate. It was the target for looting on a mass scale; a free for all. Although it wasn't ramraided, it was as a consequence of a ramraider being arrested that the raid took place.

January 1992 – The showcase shopping centre of the north-east had become a hunting ground for these new-age raiders. Marks & Spencer at the Metro Centre was at the rear end of a vehicular attack and suffered some £1,500 worth of damage in the process. As usual, the raiders were becoming pretty effective in committing the crime and escaping into the dead of night without detection. A sophisticated CCTV system was being rigged up by M & S, but well after the horse had bolted from its stable! We had a recession on and the thieves were going to take advantage of the apparently inadequate security system M & S, and other retailers, had in place.

May 1992 – Here we have a successful raid with a poor end result for one of the raiders. It was obvious that the law would come down heavy on whoever was caught, for any type of ramraid no matter how small. Fuck me, they might as well throw away the key to the cell. Aaron Trotter of Washington paid his dues when up in front of the 'Domino King' Judge Dennis Orde. Judge Orde had become known as 'The Domino King' due to the way he would pass sentence: 'Hmmmm! I think I will give you three years, but then again I might make it four, but considering the circumstances I might make it two, of course I could give you ten years.' As it happens, Aaron Trotter was given a rather strange total of two-and-a-half years for his part in a ramraid.

Trotter of Trotter's Independent Ramraid company played a part in a bingo-hall ramraid! A fucking bingo-hall ramraid? The Regal Bingo Hall in Concorde, Washington had suffered thousands of pounds' worth of damage when raiders drained the contents from gaming machines. The meagre amount stolen was overshadowed by the damage, estimated at some nine grand! The proceeds amounted to a few hundred quid – he deserved to be caught by the sound of it. The police had a reasonably easy job when they found the – empty – cash boxes in the home of Wayne Moody; he received nine months in Her Majesty's Hotel (HM Prison Durham) for the pleasure.

February 1995 – Yes, we've moved on a couple of years. Rather than bore you with a whole catalogue of raids, we move on otherwise you'll not get to read the end of the book because we'll run out of space. Way back in 1992, the law had a break in nicking the biggest gang of ramraiders this side of the Mason–Dixie line. We'll expand on the 1992 situation later on when we speak to Faggo, one of the leading suspects and pains in the arse of Northumbria Police Force. In fact, I would guess this is what helped turn the then Chief Constable, Stanley Bailey's, hair grey.

Previous ramraiders used the strategy of raiding the same place twice within hours. The technique certainly added to their haul of goodies, and this also applied to the raid near to the good old Metro Centre. Outdoor World was to offer up its succulent goods to the skills of the ramraider. Years previously, in 1993, the store had been victim to a rather clever trick employed by the raiders. A protective bollard had been torn out. The police had attended but soon left the scene and the raiders cleared up their haul. Now we would see the store targeted once more. Plenty of goods for the occupants of west Gateshead to get their hands on in the confines of neon-lit smoke-filled pubs. The police were berated for leaving the scene of the crime.

February 1995 – A liquor store had its rear wall caved in by virtue of a vehicle running through it – nothing was taken in this failed raid.

March 1995 – Singh's store in Red House, Sunderland suffered a loss of cigarettes in a successful raid.

August 1995 – Here we have another retired pro-footballer going into the retail trade: wonder why?

Just out of interest, we had John 'Budgie' Burridge, the former Newcastle United goalkeeper, up before the beak for trading in snide gear – counterfeit branded sportswear – but that's another story, although he was given a substantial fine imposed at a magistrates' court for the pleasure of handling the fake gear. Budgie was the victim of a covert operation by Trading Standards officers.

Back to the story – here we have ex-Nottingham Forest pro-footballer Peter Harrison setting himself up a little business. The shop, not surprisingly, was going to be selling designer leisurewear. Before the shop was opened to the public it was the victim of a ramraid; the little shop, on Gateshead's Saltwell Road, was soon emptied of £2,000 worth of clothes. Judging by the price tags on some of the designer clothes for sale in this type of shop, I reckon two carrier bags would have been the lot in this little raid. Peter didn't bother opening the shop and his venture was cancelled, which would lose the rundown area a much-needed pick-me-up.

October 1995 – A raid with a difference. Musically minded raiders got away with a small amount of musical equipment on a raid at a Whitley Bay shop, The Home Organ Centre to be exact. These highly talented raiders can now be heard blasting away the mandatory 'ticki-toh, boom, boom, tick-a-tah', which can be heard emanating from most cars driven by the 'hot hatch' brigade. You would think that the tape playing this stuff was mandatory to use. I'd like to hear them whistle the same tunes when away from their one-ton mobile tape player.

August 1998 – Let's move on just a little, as I think you might now be getting the picture of what was going on in the north-east in terms of ramraids. The favourite items that attracted raiders, like magpies are attracted to silver, was once again in the news. A raid on the LD Mountain Centre in Newcastle's Dean Street was carried out with the swiftness of an Exocet missile travelling around Saddam Hussain's HQ.

The steel roller shutters crumpled like butter in the sun under the firepower of a Land Rover reversing at full pelt into them, tearing them off their mounts and continuing through a plate-glass window the size of a barn door. As the shutter was swinging like a pendulum, the gang moved in a way that would have had the most seasoned shoplifter looking on with envy. 'To me.' 'To you.' 'To me.'

In a flash, some £25,000 worth of branded goods was removed from the heaving shelves and the hangers of display rails. Considering CCTV cameras were and still are operating in Newcastle, they did not act as a deterrent; the urge was just too great. The shop where Chris Bonnington had once shopped was now a barren and desolate place – just like the top of Mount Everest.

Such a raid was well planned; a foot soldier would go into the shop during opening hours and goods would be earmarked for the raid. Cheaper branded goods would be ignored as more attractively priced items would sell on the black market quicker – they had their punters to think of. Damage to the premises was considerable; such trivia was of no interest to the gang and the damage was a means to an end. Given the location of the premises and its contents, earlier ramraids had not been used as an example for the owners to learn from.

September 1998 – The die-hard brigade were still at it when £4,000 worth of damage was caused after a garage was hit in a ramraid of small proportions. A fuel station in Birtley, near to Chester-le-Street, was raided in order to get at a small amount of goods in what was probably more an act of bravado than a real raid of epic proportions.

CHAPTER TWO

SETTING THE TREND

IN JULY 1991, ramraiding in the north-east of England was to become curtailed somewhat when police launched Operation Jugular. This was designed to bring the raiding spree to an end. Seventy police officers from the Northumbria Police Force were involved in what they called 'undercover surveillance'. In reality it all boiled down to one disgruntled person bringing the ramraiding jamboree to an end for one hardcore gang – more on that later. The fashion moguls in London usually set trends; here the roles were reversed. The ramraiding phenomenon was set to take hold of the rest of the country.

Ramraiding had been run out of town and it was now the turn of others to emulate a trend that had thwarted the best cops in the region. The gang had been smashed by the carelessness of a gang member in not paying his catalogue payment to a 16-year-old girl. Skill and stupidity rolled into one; all geniuses have some sort of a flaw and, as much as that is true, there's also something called 'the compulsion to confess' in all of us. The need to leave a clue or make something happen so as to be caught. It's instilled into us all from day one: 'Don't touch', 'Put it back, that's naughty', 'You naughty, naughty ...', 'You must tell the truth', 'If I catch you doing ...' and so on. Let's see what was going on around the country in a few randomly selected incidents.

April 1992 – The ramraid gang now firmly locked away in high-security prisons could set about promoting the idea to fellow cons. No one could accuse the raiders of doing things by half when a stolen skip wagon was used to ram into a building society. The Nationwide Anglia at Cranleigh in Surrey was to become a trendsetter for others to copy, in that the skip wagon was used to wrench the cash machine out of the ground. Chains were quickly attached to the sturdy steel structure of the cash machine and with a heave-ho it was yanked out of its concrete-embedded mountings.

The cash machine was now swinging precariously on the chains as the wagon drove off with its booty loosely attached. Fucking hell, the whole thing slipped off the chains and it careered down the road making a clattering noise that would awaken nearby residents.

The startled gang continued driving, dumped the wagon and made off in a stolen Ford Transit van. Oh well, plenty more where that came from!

April 1992 – A couple of weeks later, a rather larger and more powerful vehicle was used in a similar type of ramraid to the one mentioned above. As mentioned above, a JCB is one of those big yellow/green machines with a mechanical arm at the back and a big fuck-off bucket at the front. They are usually driven by protégés of Michael Schumacher at speeds of up to 20mph in the overtaking lane along dual carriageways in the rush hour.

A JCB was taken from a nearby site and the raid happened at 3.30am. The victim this time would be the Abbey National in the Hempstead Valley Shopping Centre, near Gillingham, Kent; a nice clean operation with no slip-ups was to see the removal of the cash machine. Previous raids in the south-east of London had seen a wide range of heavy plant equipment used, a forklift and a bulldozer being just a couple.

These cash machines offered up substantial amounts of cash, which meant there was no nasty middleman needed to sell designer-labelled clothes to. Cash was a far easier commodity to shift, especially if you were down the pub or in the bookies. These raids had caught the southern constabularies off their guard, just as with those in the northern police forces.

April 1992 – No sooner was it mentioned that the

'Hole in the Wall' gang had achieved success than a patrolling policeman accidentally stumbled across an early-morning ramraid in progress at the much-favoured Abbey National building society at Romford in east London. It seemed too good to be true for one young PC.

'Oy, you're nicked, sunshine!' The young PC abandoned his vehicle and gave chase on foot, catching one of the gang and then radioing for assistance. As a consequence, other officers arriving at the scene picked up two further gang members nearby. There's always one that gets away and that was the case here; no doubt he lives to tell the tale of how he escaped capture while being a member of the 'Hole in the Wall' gang.

When you consider that the machines usually held some £60,000, it's not surprising that these tantalising cash dispensers attracted the attentions of such gangs. Previous raids had netted some £200,000 smackers! The cash machines were torn from their mountings with ease by powerful machines – like taking candy from a baby.

The Easter Sunday of 1992, a few weeks prior to the above incident, this holy day had its peace disturbed by a gang using a forklift to barge their way into the Abbey National at Gillingham, Kent. The haul secured £57,000 smackers! The idea was to rip the dispenser out and then to load it on to a much faster vehicle and get the hell out of there – a method that was to be applied time and time again.

Previous raids on Abbey National branches at Tulse Hill, Sutton, Peckham and Bromley had prompted the directors of Abbey National to offer a £20,000 reward for the capture of the gang. These raids prompted other financial institutions throughout the country with hole-in-the-wall dispensers to review security.

June 1992 – What was lost in finesse was more than made up for by the ramraiders in their impeccable taste for high fashion. Femme, a village high-street shop, fell victim to the fashion-conscious ramraiders. The fashion shop based in Sunninghill, Berkshire was geared up to supply the ladies of the toffs intending to attend Royal Ascot Race Day – only the raiders got there first, a few days before Berkshire was to see the annual parading of such labels as Trina Lewis, Gina Baconi, Shubette and Slimma – what a fucking shame that the jetset were going to be deprived of the chance to strut their stuff.

Some 200 dresses and separates were taken. The shop owner said, 'The ramraiders knew what they were looking for as they ignored all of the cheap T-shirts.' A value of £35,000 was put on the stolen stock. Similar raids had taken place some years previous to this in the north-east, when bridalwear shops were targeted in the dead of night. And in one raid the whole contents of a furniture showroom was cleared up!

January 1994 – The ramraid craze was spreading faster than a vicar leaping from the window of a brothel during a police raid. Bristol's little cherubs soon cottoned on to the idea of using a car as a door opener. Twelve houses were burgled when raiders used the corner of the boot to smash open doors of dwelling homes. True professionals take a seriously bad view of dwelling-house burglary. Certain houses were targeted, particularly of those who worked for a living. Such raids netted small hauls but had big consequences for the victims.

September 1994 – Land Rovers were fast becoming popular with ramraiders and here we have an example of what I can see as the only good use for such a vehicle. Here in the UK, drive around any car park and what do you see if you wait long enough? Some slightly built female driving an extension of her husband's penis. Watch long enough and you might even get to see one of them manage to park such a vehicle in the space that three juggernauts would take up. The biggest, most useless tool I have ever come across – after owning three of them myself, I'm cured now.

Metal bollards in place at the Kingstanding pedestrian area in Birmingham were as much use as matchsticks when a Land Rover ploughed through them and then into the side wall of a crowded Post Office. The wall collapsed like a house of cards and with that the gang were able to enter from the staff side of the counter. Only minutes earlier a delivery of cash had been dropped off at the Post Office.

All was going well up to the point when the gang produced water pistols and squirted a noxious liquid at the crowd of customers. The caustic liquid stopped people in their tracks; their eyes streamed tears as the raiders squirted people in a blind panic to get away, which they did with some £100,000. A well-planned operation, spoiled by needless and brutal actions, made this a top-shelf raid – one to be avoided.

March 1995 – In contrast to the above raid, we have the real McCoy here. The Securicor depot at Bolton, Greater Manchester suffered a £400,000 loss when ramraiders used a tipper lorry to ram through its brick wall. As cool as a cucumber, two masked men carrying sawn-offs approached staff demanding cash – they were duly rewarded with enough money to buy a couple – well, nearly – of McLaren F1s.

February 1998 – Oh yes, they are still at it. Our favourite, the Land Rover, is being used once more for what it was best designed for. An Adisham clothes warehouse was ramraided in the early hours. The Hydra Clothes company suffered damage and losses in this basic raid. When police tailed the Land Rover, it was driven at them in reverse and eventually made a getaway; to be found later, dumped and on fire.

September 1998 – West Orchards shopping centre, Coventry was not alone in being ramraided. Various shopping centres throughout the UK have suffered similar attacks. Tyneside's showpiece Metro Centre shopping complex, often vying to be the largest in Europe, suffered at the hands of ramraiders; Durham's much smaller Milburngate shopping centre also suffered such a raid, although the gang were unsuccessful in stealing goods.

Such rites of passage were reserved for only the best and the West Orchards centre had now come of age. This raid stands out as one of only a few that can be considered legendary and would certainly attract kudos and respect of a very high standard among fellow ramraiders. The planning of such a raid will be looked at later on when we get to hear what a top-notch ramraider says of such operations.

In this raid, two stolen cars were used. A Ford Escort estate would be the battering vehicle. The early hours of the morning, 3.30, would see the first floor being raided. Access to the first floor was gained via a pedestrian ramp from Broadgate. First the bollard blocking vehicular access up the ramp was dispensed with. Mainly being for cosmetic purposes, this bollard was like papier-mâché. No problemo, now up the ramp and smashing the complex's doors into oblivion didn't seem to present a problem.

The target was the Eltex fashion shop; the sound of the Escort estate's revving engine echoed around the mall and, within an instant, the shop was opened –

like a sardine can. The second vehicle, a Ford Escort saloon, was loaded up and they were off. The estate car having done its job was left in a mangled mess, as if in some symbolic salute to the skills of its now absent driver.

From start to finish, this raid was a piece of precision work – five minutes. By the time the police arrived on the scene the raiders had long gone. Such artistic work was seldom seen in the annals of ramraiding and for this reason it stands apart from 99 per cent of all other raids. No one hurt, no violence threatened, no casualities – one for the purists of social history. Henry Ford never knew what he had unleashed on the world when he said, 'You can have any colour car you want, as long as it's black!'

October 1998 – An agricultural equipment supplier, Thurlow Nunn Standen, at Kenford, near to Newmarket, was to suffer damage in a foiled ramraid. Again, opportunely, police were nearby when the gates of the compound were rammed in such a way as to allow entrance through a side wall into the supplier's premises. Sitting nearby, parked at the village shop, was a police car occupied by two officers.

The police gave chase but were rammed by the stolen Toyota pickup truck used in the raid. A police helicopter and tracker dogs were used to search for the raiders.

August 1999 – The 'Hole in the Wall' gang are at it

again in this ramraid at Tesco in Hook, Hants. An old estate car was used to batter its way through the glass doors of the food store. The cashpoint dispenser containing some £83,000 was ripped out of the wall and has never been seen again.

September 1999 – Not a ramraid for the purists this one, maybe not even an intended ramraid. A gang of teenage girls and boys decided to have a bit of fun; they slashed a man with a knife and threatened two women when they carried out four different raids on houses.

They used a stolen car to ramraid the door of a house in Cornfield, Stalybridge, leaving damage estimated at £1,000. That wasn't the end of their spree, as it was soon apparent that they would be up to no good when confronted by a man defending his property. He soon got verbally assaulted and retreated indoors. They followed and he was slashed across the leg with a knife, his car keys and other goods were taken and later on his car, a Honda Civic, was found dumped in Manchester.

The same gang is thought to have assaulted an elderly woman at her isolated farmhouse, from which jewellery was taken. Another incident involved the gang in taxing a woman of her car. OK, it wasn't classed as a proper ramraid, but it goes to show how cars can play a role in crime that leads on to other more serious incidents. Women are becoming more aggressive and are taking part in more serious types of crime than previously thought possible. But remember this, women receive longer prison sentences in comparison to those that men receive for the same crime, and the chances of a woman being sent to prison are now deemed to be higher than that of a man.

'Hell hath no fury like a woman scorned' (try to remember that phrase for later). Was it a woman who said that? Who knows? Clare Madine attacked her ex-lover and chewed off his ear! Madine and her ex accused each other of cheating and, as a consequence, she waited for him at his secluded country home in Northumberland. The ear couldn't be sewn back on and Madine was given a suspended prison sentence.

Emma Moore gave her ex something to think about – a knee in the balls! Her ex needed stitches and may have suffered in the fertility stakes. For whatever reason she did him, she did him well. Her price for that was a 15-month prison sentence. Her counsel at court described her as 'a delightful, sweet and delicate woman who would not normally hurt a fly'. Maybe she wouldn't hurt a fly but she certainly got her ex in the fly! What is it about women and their ex-partners? Don't answer that.

Compare that one to this act of violence. Amanda Styles burgled an elderly lady's home. The lady was 73 years old and ended up with permanent brain damage when Styles stabbed her in the head and tried to strangle her. Styles was put away for three years. Not much of a sentence when you consider what I've just written about women being treated more harshly than men have been at the law courts. Not knowing the full circumstances, though, it would be difficult to comment.

So you can see from these few examples that women are becoming that little bit more violent and are prepared to use it as and when required. What the fuck that has to do with ramraiders is for you to decide.

A point of reference that might interest you purists at heart is another title which I've written with my old sparring partner – sparring with pens, that is – Charles Bronson's *Legends*, available now. A chapter in that book is devoted to women, proving that Charlie Bronson and I are not biased against the fairer sex. Oh, sorry, I shouldn't have said that in case one of those feminists comes along and gives Charlie and me a length of her tongue – fucking hell, shouldn't have said that either. You know what I mean though.

March 2005 – Yes, ramraids are still in vogue. A digger, one of the favourite tools of a ramraid gang, was used to its full capacity when ramraiders robbed a Natwest in Borough Green, Kent. Police are currently pursuing the gang they believe have struck five times before. The day before this raid, they offered a £10,00 reward leading to their arrest and conviction.

March 2005 – In a typical, one car to ram and one

car to getaway, a ramraid gang struck in the early hours of the morning when they used a stolen Vauxhall Astra car to ram the shutters of the Heworth Metro Station concourse in Gateshead. After successfully ramming through the shutters and steel-framed, glass panelled doors; they went for the ATM cash dispenser. Although the car smashed into the machine, the ramraiders failed to get their prize, and fled empty-handed in their awaiting getaway car, leaving thousands of pounds worth of damage in their wake.

Acting Det Chief Insp Steve Binks of Gateshead police was lived when he warned that anyone trying to resurrect this ramraiding craze would be brought before the courts for tough sentencing.

I've got to sneak this one in here – for those of you in the Gateshead area of Tyneside. When I lived nearby there was this guy, I call him 'Piss off, fuck off, piss off'. He used to ride a bicycle all over Tyneside and if anyone looked at him for too long he would say, 'Piss off, fuck off, piss off.' Anyone know whom I'm on about?

CHAPTER THREE

EXPORTING THE RAMRAID PHENOMENON

THIS CHAPTER IS short, not because I couldn't find enough material to fill it but because I don't feel it bears a great relevance for my readers. OK, now I can be accused of making the decisions for you – I assure you that is not the case. You want to know what's going on around you and to be able to relate to it, and for that reason I don't fancy going into such depths as covering every single ramraid that went on around the world; we'd have a book as thick as Salman Rushdie's *Satanic Verses*, which in my opinion is a parcel of shite and I haven't even read it – hypocritical of me, isn't it? Well, he never plugs my books so why should I plug his?

Anyone been to Cyprus? No/yes, whatever, it doesn't matter. You've seen postcards of the place and the like so that's as close as you need to get to it, although it's fast becoming the place to be. They drive on the same side of the road as we do, so there's no trying to remember what side of the fucking road to drive on. The traffic signs and direction boards are in dual languages – one of which is English. And they drive just as mad, if not madder than us lot over here. You should see them when they come to a red traffic light, talk about waving a red rag in front of a bull – this is fucking war, mate. They're halfway across the stop line while the light is still on red – brilliant stuff to watch. Mind you, the speed limit is 100kmh, not 100 fucking mph as some people think so, with that in mind, it's no wonder ramraiders are doing the business over there.

Would you believe that I travelled all the way over there on a six-and-half-hour flight? (Included an hour delay because some silly fucking baggage handler had decided they'd put an Irishman's case on my aeroplane, when he was destined elsewhere, and to top it all after they'd looked for it, they decided that it wasn't even on my fucking plane!)

I had to suffer the golden beaches, lots of cheap booze, lots of cheap bargains on the markets, hot lazy days around the poolside and other painful experiences just to bring you this piece of news. What I did was to walk along the high street areas filming the windows of jewellery shops and furriers, yes, furriers. The temperature was 110 degrees in Larnaka and here we have a whole flock of shops selling fur coats – funny fuckers over there, them Cypriots. There was madness in my reasoning that if I were to film the shop windows it might arouse some action, and sure enough it did. You should have seen the shopkeepers of such outlets as Sophia Gold & Diamond come running out waving their hands about, shouting, 'No, no, no!' It was certainly obvious that they had experienced the wonders of the ramraid phenomenon; either that or they were camera shy.

I mean, there I was with my trusty piece of camera, filming away in a foreign place without giving a toss for my own safety, and then I go to the border of Southern and Northern Cyprus and start filming the bullet holes in the concrete buildings in full view of the armed border guard. There are signs splattered all around in a million different languages telling you not to film or photograph the derelict buildings that were abandoned from the north/south divide battle that took place only a few years ago.

I was spotted from one of the many border guard watchtowers and an almighty fuck-off voice starts shouting at me from the distance. I look around and I see a guard with his rifle at the ready in one of the lookout towers and I do a runner from the safety of my side of the border – let's see this geezer McIntyre do that. Me, I had my dirty big Sony on my shoulder. Cook/McIntyre, who gives a toss? Me, I do, I give a toss, as you are all being short-changed out there. I was going to go over the border to interview a guy called Asil Nadir.

Asil fucked off from the UK while on a few million quid bail; he's now in Northern Cyprus. He used to run a company called Polypeck and some sort of fraud investigation was going on, and he was eventually charged for allegedly mishandling bucket loads of money. The thing is, he fucked off because the prosecution had come into possession of all of his defence papers when the police raided and took all the paperwork relating to his defence away from him. This guy Nadir was no ordinary guy and I believe he could have spilled the beans on a lot of high-placed people over here.

So the prosecution sees his defence papers when the police hand it over and, hey presto, he has no other option but to fuck off. What would you do?

He's got publishing interests in Northern Cyprus and he's still got a few million quid so it was no big deal for him.

Anyway, I didn't have the opportunity to see him as a bomb was thrown at the police headquarters in Larnaka while I was there, so I was off looking for the local Mafia. They'd bombed the doors off the police station to let them know they weren't going to take things lying down, as the police had clamped down on the local Mafia. Then one of the border guards was shot. It was rumoured he had shot himself to get off guard duty, and there's me filming away around these trigger-happy cunts! I was filming for my own personal reference library, as I never know when these sorts of things will come in handy. Asil is featured in a book Charlie Bronson and I have put out. The book, mentioned above, is called *Legends*. It's a real eye opener, so if Asil hears about this I want him to get me an interview so we can spill the beans on all them high-up people that look down on you and me.

Remember what I said about those fur coats? Well, here goes.

24 December 1998 – One of the furriers I mentioned had its comeuppance when ramraiders struck on Christmas Eve. A Kato Paphos fur shop, Orstias Fur Shop, was rammed by a stolen Colt saloon car, which was left at the scene in a usual two-car raid – one to ram and one to gan away quickly. The raid, in which three men snatched six mink coats, took place at the favoured time of around 3am.

If this was in the UK then maybe we could accuse the Animal Liberation Front of having some involvement, but this was in Cyprus and these were real cool mink coats. Can you imagine somebody's granny swanking around Newcastle in one of these pieces? Grey's Club here we come! The only person I know that would have bought one would have been

John Lennon, or maybe one of the Hell's Angels chapters that runs around Matlock Bath, Derbyshire.

The value of the coats was estimated at £9,000 (sterling) and to top it all, the shop was actually insured. When you consider that you can pick up one of these relics from a Women's Institution jumble sale for about a fiver it might well be worth taking a few over there to flog.

New Zealand – An island where lamb chops are plentiful and parrots are as big as eagles. In a way it makes sense, as the Kea parrot swoops down on lambs – mhhhhh, nice with some mint sauce. So an island full of sheep and lamb-eating parrots would seem to be the sort of place any hard-boiled clean-living person would want to settle in and take it easy, watching the goings on from the serenity of their balcony: parrots, lambs and ramraiders! Yes, ramraiders.

January 1999 – The Richmond mall was the target for raiders to strike at: the prize – a cash dispenser full of money. As usual, the use of some heavy-lifting gear is going to be needed so the old favourite, a forklift truck, is employed along with the mandatory second vehicle to load the dispenser into. The stolen Datsun pickup was driven into the mall at 3am, closely following the forklift, which had penetrated the flimsy protection afforded by glass doors.

The Westpac Trust ATM machine was pulled out of

the ground with ease, but the alarm was going off and the raiders seemed to have lost their co-ordination and, whoops, the machine fell to the floor. Nothing for it but to make themselves scarce before it all came on top. They left empty handed. The pickup truck disappeared into the dark of night with its lights out. The damage to the mall was extensive and an estimated cost of £10,000 was put at repairing the frontage and the drive motors for the doors. Although the police planned raids on the homes of suspects, it seemed as though a lot was based on guesswork. What else did they have to go on? As with most police investigations, obviously the mere act of guessing would not catch the team involved; this sort of thing was best left to the police informer. Later on we'll see how a main gang of ramraiders from the north-east of England were caught by the use of police informants.

Australia is the furthest place away from the UK if we remain on Earth, so if ramraiding was to be exported as far away as that then it could truly be recognised as an international crimewave.

1998 – Seems to have been a very good year for ramraiding. Too many raids happened during this time to be able to give you a full listing. Some 150 ramraids took place in Sydney, Australia! It was estimated that the losses attributed directly to ramraids were a minimum of A$5 million; this figure is the wholesale costings in an 18-month period so you can imagine what the retail values would have been.

The favoured outlets to be graced by the presence of ramraiders were the off-airport duty-free outlets. No prizes for guessing what the raiders were after from these places. Retail premises were being attacked systematically and at will, and the traders joked bitterly about which city store would be next on the ramraiders' list. It was fair to say that any store with a street frontage could face the prospect of at least having an attempt made on it.

Part of the Nuance group, City International Duty Free stores, were hit seven times in as many months and, of course, the items targeted were always designer-wear watches, such as Tag Heuer, which had a high profile among younger buyers.

So there you have it, hard evidence that ramraids were an export from Newcastle upon Tyne to the furthest part of the world – what a feat to achieve. When you consider that there is also a 'Newcastle' in Australia, maybe it's not a coincidence.

Maybe it can be said that because news travels so fast, and because we are more in touch with world news and events, this could be the reason for the rest of the world copying such a crime – I think so, yes!

Maybe I can get James Nicholson, the Old Bailey Court Reporter known as 'Le Prince', to chase this one up. Read about Le Prince and his friendship with the late Valerio Viccei ('A tribute to Gi Gi') in *Legends*, written by Charlie Bronson – some good photos of them together.

CHAPTER FOUR

WACKY, WEIRD & ODD

ALL OF THE items that follow have taken place over a number of years, right up to the present time of writing, but I have decided not to date them or put them in any particular order. Previous chapters have been compiled in that way, but I don't want you becoming bored with the set-up, so let's change the flow a little.

Melons and things that go bump in the night – A ramraid gang thought that a supermarket would be a pushover, no sweat. As usual, the target in such a place was the cashpoint machine. But what should have been an easy job turned a little sour.

A stolen Mitsubishi Shogun and a turbo-charged Volvo estate crashed through the front doors of the Tesco store in New Malden, Surrey. The Shogun was first reversed through the glass doors, followed by the

Volvo, while a third vehicle waited nearby. The five-man gang had not, though, taken into account the bravery of shelf-stackers working away. Hiding behind the shelves were the night-shift staff, ordinary folk making an honest living. When they saw what was about to happen, they started pelting the raiders with a variety of goods.

The initial terror caused by the noise and glass being showered everywhere had subsided. The night shift, about a hundred of them, were beginning to collect their senses. They started throwing melons, pomegranates, kiwi fruits, prickly pears and vegetables; although the masked gang were armed with baseball bats, it didn't deter the staff from bombarding the gang with fruit, rather like the old stocks of medieval times – the rogues were pelted with rotten fruit and veg.

Initially the Shogun had repeatedly rammed the cash machine and what looked like being a successful raid was U-turned by the combined force of a quick-thinking workforce.

One of the gang was hit on the head with a melon and at this point the ammunition being used was being lobbed from all quarters – time for a sharp exit. The gang certainly didn't expect to be met with such a barrage and what should have been an easy job turned into a melon-choly evening for the baseball-bat-wielding raiders. What could have been a rather nasty incident was avoided by these professionals. It would have been easy for them to use their weapons but, as mentioned previously, true ramraiders wouldn't risk an extra ten stretch being added on to their prison sentences because violence was used, and for that reason this gang must be given some credit.

Dick Turpin/Ned Kelly, Stand and Deliver – For those of you too young to remember the days when Dick Turpin of England and Ned Kelly of Australia were around some couple of centuries ago, I will explain. They were legendary characters: highwaymen, robbers, muggers and criminals; some of the first pavement artists of their time. Turpin would be on his horse and chase after a carriage carrying the rich. He'd pull out his pistols and shout, 'Stand and deliver!' If the carriage stopped, which invariably it did, he'd take items of value and, of course, cash. Ned Kelly had this big fuck-off metal mask and breast shield in case he was shot; maybe the first bulletproof vest.

How the fuck does Dick Turpin and Ned Kelly come into this story? Modern-day highway robbers still exist! An incident in which two men boxed in an elderly couple's Volvo car with their own turned nasty. After boxing in the car, both men got out and smashed the driver's and the passenger's door windows of the Volvo, in Norwich Avenue, Elm Tree, Stockton in the dusky evening of November.

The elderly couple, pensioners, were held to ransom and the woman's handbag was snatched, leaving both victims shocked and horrified. A bit of a let-down in the ramraid stakes, but this was not a true ramraid so maybe we can let true raiders off the hook – for now that is.

Van Gone: The Ramraid Artist – What were considered to be six of the world's most expensive paintings were stolen by ramraiders. Among the haul were paintings by Van Gogh and Picasso valued at £100 million. Treasures were systematically plundered from a bank in Holland, two museums in France and, would you believe it, a yacht berthed at Antibes on the French Riviera, all over a period of a year.

The gang's method of entry was very crude but very effective – reversing a van through the windows of chateaux and museums. Although using crude methods, the gang was a pro outfit, avoiding CCTV cameras as if they were the plague. Selective in what they took, they went through the place at the speed of a Stealth Bomber.

This gang of ramraiders beats all other gangs hands down for the total value of goods per raid. Police hunting the gang claim that paintings and other artefacts are stolen to order for the Mafia. Even bigger claims suggest that the gang is a bunch of gypsies. We thought the cash-dispenser operation was the one to reap the biggest haul for ramraiders but this slick operation shows how far ramraiding can be taken; a far cry from ramming some little gaff in Newcastle upon Tyne, England.

Ram-a-person – Ramraiding, as we've seen above, was taken a few steps up the ladder, but this story takes the ramraiding phenomenon down a peg or two. A car rammed a dear old lady, 77 years old. As she lay on the road, the ramraider snatched her handbag. OK, maybe a one-off. No! A few minutes later the same ploy was used on an even older lady – 82 years old. Naming the ladies would only add to their pain and suffering.

The 82-year-old lady was walking to attend her birthday party, which was being held at a church hall in Liverpool. This dear old lady gallantly fought off the weirdo and bravely held on to her bag as she lay on the ground. The 77-year-old lady suffered a broken pelvis and cracked ribs. Brave fuckers these types of ramraider, eh? Little old ladies should be left alone and so should little old men, come to that. 'Granny bashing' is a fucking ugly crime and the consequences of such actions will follow the perpetrators around for the rest of their lives, especially if fellow inmates in prison find out!

Six other pensioners, all OAPs, were hurt when it is thought that the same thug robbed them of their bags by snatching them through his car window – what a hero! As far as I can make out, he wasn't caught for these attacks but somewhere along the line he'll get his comeuppance, that's for sure.

We all, each of us, live in our own insular world, hearing, via the media, what goes on around us. God forbid it ever happens to us and so the world passes us by on a conveyor-belt full of other people's troubles and strifes. So what if some big department store gets ramraided? So what if it goes on right under our own nose? Until it happens to us, then nothing can prepare us for the likely consequences.

Sometimes we have to stop and take a look at what's going on with regard to what is likely to happen to *us*, as opposed to what is likely to happen to others. We can all fall victim to this sort of brutal attack; we've no recompense from large insurance companies, Criminal Injuries Board payments are puny and the little cherubs that do this sort of thing don't give a toss. At times we have to rely on the benevolence of others in order to restore our dignity after suffering such abuse. Anyone who wishes to prey on the weak and helpless can always expect some sort of return on his or her investment – remember that! When their bank account's full – wham!

On Yer Bike, Mate – Some ramraiders don't seem to know their arse from their elbow. In this raid, a stolen van smashed its way through the wall of a cycle shop shop situated at Gilesgate, Durham. The van was stolen only minutes earlier in this rather senseless and wasteful raid.

Would you believe that the raiders rode away on cycles pulled from the mangled mess they left behind? The mountain bikes stolen were rather expensive but it seemed like they were using a sledgehammer to crack open a walnut; so much effort for so little return.

Ram-out-of-a-Jam – There you are driving along nice and easy and some idiot pulls out in front of you from a side road. He has to be an idiot because he pulls out directly in front of a law car! 'OK, officer, my foot slipped off the brake when I saw your lovely coloured car, I was distracted.' Maybe that could have been a defence, but when the police give chase the Ford Sierra stops and reverses into the front of the law car, not once but twice. 'Sorry, officer, but your flashing blue disco lights blinded me and I couldn't see what gear I was in.' Definitely not a defence. The car, occupied only by the driver, does a shoot.

The police officers, a man and a woman, suffered whiplash injuries in this motiveless car-to-car encounter. The car was later found abandoned in nearby Houghton-le-Spring, Tyne & Wear. This sort of thing is usually an act of bravado brought on by too much testosterone in the system of an overactive young 'un. The other game is called 'chicken'. I'm sure my readers will know what this is; after all, I don't want to be accused of having to explain the far end of a fart, but you would be surprised how many people haven't a clue what 'chicken' is. Judges are the best characters for not knowing what such simple things are. They do seem a little detached, especially after I've watched a number of them make spectacles of themselves. You can imagine some barrister in a Crown Court saying to a judge, 'M'Lord, the defendant was playing chicken ...' The judge intervenes, 'What's "chicken"?' Need I go on?

Here's one for you: I was at Luton Crown Court for Charlie Bronson's hostage-taking trial. Well, I thought I'd bring the media's attention to Charlie's plight so I thought up a stunt, which was funny. It actually happened, and was designed to draw serious attention to the claims Charlie was and still is making of brutality by the system. Charlie used to make demands for blow-up dolls when he'd taken a hostage inside prison; of course, it was his own way of attracting media attention to his prison plight.

So there I was standing outside Luton Crown Court, blowing up four blow-up dolls! The media was around us so it seemed like a fine time to get the publicity machine into operation. I was stood there with a whole host of people looking on in varying degrees of amusement or shock. As it happens, some six months previous, I'd pulled the same stunt outside London Weekend Television Centre; I even took that doll into the boardroom of the head of documentaries and it took pride of place at the head of the table, taking notes of course!

Anyway, back to the Luton Crown Court stunt. It was a serious attempt to focus on the brutality Charlie Bronson has endured over the years while in prison. I was the only one to cook up such ideas and all went well, but it could have gone something like this (although it didn't):

"Ello, 'ello, 'ello, what's going on 'ere then? You're nicked for a "Section 5" [Public Order Offence], would you mind accompanying me to the station, sir?'

So I end up in front of the judge and the prosecution says, 'Your Honour, Richards had with him an autobiography of Charles Bronson ...'

The judge breaks in, 'What is an autobiography?'

This is explained to him and the prosecution goes on, 'Richards also had a Bronsonmania pen ...'

'Stop,' says the judge. 'What is a "Bronsonmania pen?" This too is explained to him.

The prosecution continues, 'Richards had with him four blow-up dolls ...'

Again the judge intervenes and we all expect the judge to say his usual 'what's a ...', but he doesn't. Instead he says, 'Was it the standard or the Deluxe blow-up doll?'

All of the above is true except for me being nicked and going to court.

Truck Off – Jealousy is damaging. Revenge and

jealousy, though, are very dangerous when joined together. A seven-ton flatbed truck was used to repeatedly ram a council house in an attack of jealousy. Jason Allen had alleged he spotted his wife leave a club with another man. He'd assumed the worst.

Allen had decided that he'd endured enough. He cracked up. He reversed his truck at speed through the garden wall and into the house where his wife was staying, leaving walls crumbling around the seven people inside – children were among those seven.

The flatbed wagon was left embedded into the wall like a dart in a board. Luckily for those inside, the walls didn't collapse and Allen was arrested for his 15 minutes of fame. The incident happened at Newark, Nottingham, and at Nottingham Crown Court Allen was given a three-year prison sentence for his momentary loss of control, for recklessly endangering life and for damage to the council house. Allen was the brother-in-law of 16-year-old Fred Barras, the youngster shot and killed while he burgled a Norfolk farmhouse way back in 1999. Did he deserve it?

Supergran – Corbridge is a quiet place in Northumberland and a bit off the beaten track for the police to patrol. Ramraiders decided to take advantage of the generous amount of time they thought they'd have in which to get away with a ramraid on a menswear shop beneath the flat of Brenda Walker, a super-fit karate black belt.

Supergran Brenda sent the raiders packing after they had crashed a stolen car through the shop window in the early hours. Quick-thinking Brenda soon put an end to the raid by pelting the raiders with cobblestones and silver paint. She gave them a pasting they'd never forget and by time the police had arrived on the scene they'd made a sharp exit. 'Beware of supergrans in rural places' was a warning sent out. I don't think they'll be back, as is usually the case.

Road Rage: does it exist? What's such a heavy subject doing in this section, you may well wonder. Whatever the media decide to give a label to will remain like shit on a blanket. Shopping Rage, Air Rage, Trolley Rage, Smokers – I Want a Fag Rage, you name it rage. But there's something mysterious about the transformation that takes place when ordinary folk get behind the wheel of a vehicle. Ordinary mortals are transformed into godlike creatures with mystical powers that help them see through dense fog, help them know that there isn't any traffic around that blind bend, and can also make them a better driver than anyone else. And anyone who disagrees with them will get their ear bitten off!

Gloucestershire, land of the mysterious big cat, Fred West territory and home to the Crime Through Time Museum in Newent, seems a nice enough place to transform the most careful of drivers into a raging bull, and this was the case when a family of four – a man, his wife and two young daughters – were driving their Vauxhall Cavalier down an unclassified road near Coleford in the Forest of Dean. A nice day out for this family, who lived nearby in Coleford.

Whatever happened, it caused a following Ford Sierra to weave from side to side on the road from Coleford to Parkend. Eventually the two occupants of the Sierra caught up with the Cavalier and set about the family man. Both men kicked and punched the helpless victim and his ear was bitten off. Even though his wife intervened, the attack didn't stop and she was also injured. The injured couple's children were sheltering in the car and as the two assailants drove off they rammed the Cavalier, leaving one of the children injured.

Two hospitals failed to reattach the victim's ear. These assailants were a nasty piece of work; no hard man worth his salt would carry out such an attack in front of a victim's family like these two did. I've come across the hardest men you'd ever wish to meet and none of them would do such a thing; in fact, it was a pity that the Cavalier wasn't driven by such a hard case – bit of a surprise for them, don't you reckon? What if someone like Roy Shaw, author of *Pretty Boy*, was driving the car!!!!!!

Misfits of society carry out road rage of this type

and no amount of stopping them driving would change their characteristics or behaviour patterns. Cars are one of the most persuasive of machines made by man to alter the way we behave, but drastic changes can only occur in those people who are already flawed or psychologically damaged. There are a few exceptions but I'm not qualified to write on such matters. So the next time you're followed down a country lane by some maniac or maniacs in a car weaving from side to side, make sure you've got your wits and Roy Shaw about you, as it's not a road-rage culprit but a raving fucking maniac that needs to be certified.

Rage of the Roses – I've seen quite a lot of these people down souf (south), running across busy dual carriageways with bunches of roses, selling them to motorists who are stuck in traffic jams. It looks as if every male driver's a target for such flower sellers, as if he's got a nagging wife waiting at home to be calmed.

I must admit that, in the course of travelling around Surrey, Middlesex and Sussex (east and west), I've been far too preoccupied with watching the roads for my turn-off to be bothered with such sales tactics, but it can piss you off, so not surprisingly if this happened to you every night on the way home it would become a little bit of an overkill.

A business expert from Uxbridge, Middlesex, Christopher Bromham, 36, cracked when he was asked if he'd like to smell a rose while he was stuck in heavy traffic in Weybridge, Surrey. Bromham made it clear that he didn't want to sniff the rose. That should have been the end of it, but didn't the stupid flower guy go and swear at Bromham for not wanting to inhale the bouquet from such a wondrous piece of nature?

So didn't Bromham go and do something even more stupid? He stabs the flower guy in the chest! (Kenny Noye keeps springing to mind; was he also pressurised by the attack made on him?) The victim, John Peters, was kicked about the head as he went down. Emergency surgery saved Peters's life.

Bromham received a six-year prison sentence at Guildford Crown Court and was told by the recorder, 'You stabbed him and walked away.' OK, 'fair enough' you might say, but this sort of pressurised sales technique is usually applied on foreign soil. Now we're seeing more and more of it. What if someone started washing your windscreen as you moved along slowly in a traffic jam, and then they demanded payment? It's starting to happen in parts of London and is popular in the USA.

I recall a criminal-injuries claim made by a person who had been battered about the head with a lump of wood. The assailant was a man aged 70+, the victim was a 13-year-old boy. The Criminal Injuries Board stated that the boy's claim was invalid, as the old man claimed a gang that the boy was with taunted him. Even though the man admitted the offence and received a caution, the CIB turned down the boy's claim because they believed the man. Make of that what you will!

So it would be interesting to see if this man Peters is or was considered for criminal injuries on the basis of the story I've just told you, and the fact that he taunted Bromham.

Wheel have these away – When the long arm of the law is on the receiving end of vehicle crime it can serve only to show that there is no discrimination. A sports car belonging to a Chief Superintendent, who worked for Merseyside Police Force at that time, was left high and dry up on bricks when it had its wheels stolen.

The Chief Supt was attending an interview for the position of Assistant Chief Constable for the Nottingham Force. After the interview he found his Vauxhall Calibra minus the wheels and with damage to the bodywork.

The Chief Super had never been the victim of vehicle crime and he thought it was an 'audacious thing to do'. To add to that situation, he had also failed to get the job he wanted – just not his day.

Shelf Life – Remember the Tesco workers who had pelted ramraiders with fruit? Well, here is a similar occurrence of shelf-stackers using their initiative. Near to Christmas time we like to see the traditional

Christmas pudding on the shop shelves; it's a way of reminding us that it's that time of year.

Ramraiders got an early helping of Christmas pud when they raided an Asda store in Chadderton, near Oldham, Manchester. The four-member gang fled with only a few packs of cigarettes when they were pelted with Christmas puddings by shelf-stackers working late.

They're Football Crazy – A mob baying for blood surrounded the house of Manchester City's Football Club boss Peter Swales. The long-suffering chairman of Man City was paying the price of a failing football club, sixth from the bottom of the Premiership League. They were in dire straits since the former Maine Road idol, Francis Lee, had staged a hostile takeover bid after the sudden dismissal of their manager, Peter Reid. Lee, a millionaire businessman, was the arch-rival of Peter Swales, and things were heating up when fans decided to show a vote of no confidence in Swales via a number of violent acts.

During a three-month vendetta orchestrated against Swales, he became victim to all sorts of hate mail and death threats, proving that South America, Glasgow and Newcastle upon Tyne weren't the only places that people would die or kill for their football. A man can only take so much and then he either flips his lid or cracks and accepts defeat. The 87-year-old mother of Swales was being cared for in a nursing home and during a visit to her he was followed. Staff had to stop a mob of Man City supporters following him into the nursing home but some actually got as far as Swales's mother's bedside when a vigilant member of staff told them to leave or they would call the police. Fortunately, Swales's mother didn't know what was going on, and the beleaguered boss had had enough – after 20 years in power he announced his resignation.

Fans handed out leaflets informing people of the chairman's home address and this certainly caused an unduly keen interest amongst the undesirables to carry on this vendetta at Swales's home.

Where does the ramraiding connection come in? Swales owned two electrical shops in Altrincham, both of which were on the receiving end of ramraids and were badly damaged. The motive was obvious – revenge! Football's a 'funny old game', hero one minute, Antichrist the next!

So the moral of this story is, if you become a millionaire, don't devote 20 years of your life to being chairman of a football club – cos you'll get ramraided!

Ram-a-Pram-a-Ding-Dong, Thank You, Ma'am – When can ordinary prams become dangerous? When police say glass fragments could be found in them as a consequence of ramraiders reversing a stolen van into a baby-shop window, showering the prams with glass. Dangerous prams!

Police warned mums to beware of buying 'dodgy' prams because the haul would contain glass fragments. The prams stolen from Babyland in Rackheath, near Norwich were condemned as being dangerous and a police spokesman said that their experts know from experience that it's almost impossible to remove all glass from such material.

That's a very interesting fact because, you know, all of those vehicles involved in accidents in which the windscreens or other windows are broken in vehicles carrying pushchairs and the like may now unsurprisingly have extra insurance claims made for new prams and the like.

I mean, can you imagine how many people would just continue to use such things after being showered with glass even though they've been cleaned up? This opens the doors for legitimate insurance claimants to ensure the safety of their children is considered by virtue of the insurance companies.

The gang took four Mamas and Papas three-in-one Combinations and two three-wheeler buggies in a haul worth £3,000 – have you seen the price of these baby buggies? Fucking hell, you can buy a car for the same price.

Another matter is this: have you been abroad and travelled by air, yes/no? Well, if you have and you've taken a baby buggy with you then you might find it's suddenly been lost by the airline.

I can tell you there's a massive warehouse that contains many hundreds of these lost buggies, among other things. I've personally seen a whole bunch being sent by carrier to the addresses on the attached baggage labels and it makes me wonder if the baggage handlers just can't be bothered to unload them. I can imagine all of those families abroad having to buy a replacement buggy while on holiday. Maybe that's why I see so many grumpy dads abroad having to carry the young 'uns. Anyway, let's get back to the real stuff.

Fly Me to the Moon – A new concept car has been designed and tested in the USA. The project run by Moller International of California has given the 'Skycar' concept a lift. This revolutionary hovering car will be put through its paces and may become a possibility in only a few years' time. The ramraids possible with such a car are beyond imagination.

The car will be Batmobile shaped and capable of seating four people, should have a top speed of 600mph, will do 5 miles per litre of fuel and will take off and land vertically – ideal for those with a small drive. The effect this will have on the way people travel in the future will be enormous – should it get off the ground. There would be less need for pedestrianised malls, less jammed motorways and shorter journey times.

Once the concept vehicle receives a licence from the Federal Aviation Administration, anyone with a pilot's licence will be able to fly one of these in the USA. A customised hand-built version should knock you back about US$1 million. The guy behind the car is Paul Moller and he's devoted some 30 years to its development. A mass-produced model, though, is estimated to be about $60,000 and in time that might become a real possibility depending on mass sales.

Ram-a-Dam – Worshippers at a Sikh temple in a Middlesbrough red-light district are staying away because of recent troubles. Pimps and prostitutes surround the temple, where vice girls plague the nearby streets.

A priest quit after worshippers' cars were broken into, women were spoken to in a sexually suggestive manner and the temple's entrance was ramraided so as to allow burglars entry. Middlesbrough has a reasonable-sized Sikh population, therefore the temple is necessary. Middlesbrough has a 35-year tradition of having a Sikh temple, yet the Sikh community had to move to a less threatening area due to the troubles.

Middlesbrough Council were behind the religious leaders and were putting together a package for a lottery-grant application to help with relocation costs – so the temple moves away and the vice stays. Interesting the way priority is given to the vice side of things – obviously a big money spinner for the community!

FBI/CIA/NCIC/IT/MI6/MI5/CIS/CID/CDMA (Cadbury's Dairy Milk Award) – Ever had your car nicked? Yeah, bet you have. What a fucking bummer that is. There you are all ready to go to wherever, or you've been on a shopping trip to the malls, and hey presto, your car's vanished. You look around to see if it's all part of a big joke, but no – no fucker's laughing, least of all you.

The FBI in the USA use IT (Information Technology) – OK, you know what IT means, but what about my friends that haven't got a clue of such things? The only thing IT means to some of them is 'In Trouble'. Some YP ('Young Prisoner' to you) in some HMYOI (Her Majesty's Young Offenders Institution) is gonna be stuck in their pad for 23 hours in a 24-hour day and will have fuck-all to do and no access to such jiggery-pokery ideas by the Home Office. You hear about Nintendos and Gameboys being allowed into such places to act as an incentive to YPs to behave nicely. In reality, a lot of YPs go through a difficult time in these places – but how many of you want to start reading about such things when you've spent your hard-earned dosh on this little gem? I'll crack on.

The access these CIA and FBI people have to modern-day technology would blow your mind. Never mind warp factor fucking nine computers we can get our hands on, they've got access to stuff that can magnify chicken shit into the size of a full multiplex cinema screen – from a hundred miles up in the sky! They can home into digital telephone conversations faster than a seasoned ramraider can strip an electrical shop bare of its goods. The thing is they don't want anyone finding out about certain stuff they've got, and the same applies to MI5 and MI6 in the UK. I can tell you that the main telephone line to my company, Mirage Publishing, has reportedly been bugged by MI5 – someone via MI5 told me!

The FBI relies on Web interfaces to help them bust car-theft rings. The FBI call communicating with other agencies in helping them track down such rings 'mission-critical'. Law-enforcement agencies throughout the world are involved in a project called 'Vehicle File Access', which is available through the USA-based National Crime Information Center (and for those of you who don't know what NCIC stands for … well, now you do.)

Of the 1.5 million cars stolen each year in the United States, about 200,000 are shipped overseas! OK, you're not likely to see a Chevy or a Lincoln Continental on every street corner (sidewalk to you lot in the USA) in the UK, but what about the spares you can strip from one of them darn things and then go on to resell on the black market? By virtue of the stolen-car data being made available to overseas law-enforcement agencies, the FBI hopes to help officials in those countries track down criminals.

You might think there's nothing wacky or odd about that, but when you think of what the FBI usually get involved in then this seems a little off their beaten track. Isn't it a domestic problem? Why should any other country care about our stolen motor vehicles? George Saymon, a management analyst at the FBI and leader of the project in Carleston, USA, says, 'But if someone buys a stolen car, they don't buy a car from a local source in that country. Countries suffer from a lack of dynamic auto market.' Well, fancy that, what a clever clogs this guy Saymon is. What he means is that the local economy in the places where stolen cars are being sold suffers. Too fucking right it does, mate, good on you, you tell them. And will it have any effect? No!

Here's a list of the top ten most stolen cars in the USA:

Toyota Camry
Honda Accord
Honda Civic
Oldsmobile Cutlass
Jeep Cherokee/Grand Cherokee
Chevrolet Full-Size C/K pickup
Toyota Corolla
Ford Taurus
Chevrolet Caprice
Ford F150 pickup

Don't they have any Mondeos or Minis over in the States then? Nope, guess not. It would seem that pickups, sport utility vehicles, are popular with the TWOC squad in the States. If I were a Honda Accord owner in the United States I'd change my car for something less attractive, like a VW Beetle. The list above wasn't just dreamed up out of fresh air. Oh yes, there are people employed to compile such lists, would you believe. If ever that gets to be the case in the UK then please somebody give me a shout as I could name the top ten in my opinion, here with my eyes closed. We'd start with the loveable Austin series of vehicles, Ford, Vauxhall, blah, blah, blah and so on.

The NCIB's (The National Insurance Crime Bureau) data also shows that, increasingly, thieves are hauling off pickups, mini-vans and sport utility vehicles. There is no indication, though, that the thieves are being all that selective. The vehicles that are stolen most often also happen to be the vehicles bought most often. So that seems to have fucked the theory that they go for the easiest to get in and away with.

I suppose it all boils down to the theory that 'familiarity breeds contempt'. The more that's seen of one of these cars, the less likely it's going to seem hard to crack. Like taking candy from a baby, that's how the thieves look at it. Don't forget that the more popular a vehicle becomes, the more likely it will be that someone somewhere is going to want a spare part, and a cheap spare part at that.

Indeed, to car thieves, a car can be worth a lot more if it's stripped. 'The sum of the whole equals more than the value of the parts' isn't true here. 'The sum of the parts equals more than the value of the whole' is true though. So there you have it, a very interesting fact, so when your car goes missing, you can kiss it goodbye, probably, forever. Look at it rather as an organ donor; one car has prolonged the life of, maybe, 50 other cars. Maybe all cars should be fitted with donor cards.

The final subject is one close to my own heart, not because I feel it's something I'd like to do or even escape in my mind as imagining doing. It's close to my heart because one of my own lady researchers had a rather nasty experience with the driver of a BMW car. It differs slightly to what I'm going to explore in a few moments but I'll crack on and tell you about it for the moment.

My researcher's driving along when she comes to a roundabout. Sitting there is a guy, God forbid one of my own breed letting the team down. He's sitting there with a piece of plastic pushed up to his ear – should've been up his arse. It's one of those hot ear wipes, softens the wax the longer you talk into it and listen to what someone else spurts out of the little holes you've got your ear pushed up to – yes, a mobile phone (nothing personal against BMW owners, one of the best cars ever to be built).

There he is, holding the traffic up, listening to some sort of gossip. The traffic starts to pile up behind him. My researcher gives a little toot on the car horn, just a little toot, and he starts his clown act. He pulls forward and then jams his anchors on, and then he drives along a dual carriageway at 20mph on the centre line while giving great big masculine macho looks – what a fucking nonce!

Of course, by now my researcher has already pressed her auto-dial button on her phone and is able to give a commentary of what's going on using her hands-free kit. Already despatched is one of our own gorillas ready to show this clown how he should behave towards the more beautiful people among us. So she's not in the slightest bit worried; in fact, she's quite keen to see the look on this crackpot's face when he's confronted by someone willing to shake him by the throat and make him apologise and donate something to some battered woman's refuge, 'cos that's the sort of thing this type of man carries out on the weaker sex.

Should this man have decided to get out of his car and confront his victim then one can only imagine how angry a lot of our friends would have felt about such a thing happening. Not to mention that we'd have splashed his ugly face all over every book relating to crime that we ever publish, just in the interest of public awareness, mind you. We all like to think that a woman alone in her car is gonna be safe. This guy was on his own and obviously he'd had four Shredded Wheat for his breakfast that day, and must have been feeling hard as nails so as to be able to build up the courage to try to frighten a woman and endanger her life while he gets his kicks from such a mighty deed.

Our gorilla's on his way, but he has to come from three miles away and over a busy bridge. By this time he's in contact with our lady and she's able to take the car registration number, which means, if he were to do something stupid and he got away, he'd soon be traced by even more friendly gorillas. The road came to a complicated set of lanes and he fucked off; he must have sensed something was wrong due to the smile on his victim's face. He had been only a few seconds away from being collected for charity and left on the door of some woman's refuge with the words 'I hate women' tattooed on his forehead. So the next time anyone's a plonker towards a defenceless woman, they have to remember that some big gorilla might just be on his way to sort them, maybe that's why the lady's smiling at him!

Right, the final subject in this chapter – women drivers being stalked. Smash and grabs involving lone women drivers being stalked by gangs are on the increase. Who says that? The media. OK, maybe it's a little exaggerated but it does go on and has been a prominent subject in the news on a national scale. I take little heed of local news reports, regardless of which part of the UK they spout forth from. I mean, have you ever watched the news in different TV areas? Yawn, yawn.

This sort of crime isn't a new trend, it's been around for many hundreds of years. Dick Turpin was the first one to do such a thing and it will continue for the next few hundred years, except in South Africa. Have you seen those big fuck-off flame-throwers on the undersides of cars? All legal as well! 'Would you like both sides cooked, sir?' I'm not kidding, these accessories are needed to ward off car-jackers. 'Pull over, dear, that looks like a nice man, he'll help us find our way out of this jungle of streets.' Next thing you know the family have either been shot and killed, or dumped after being robbed.

So these pop-and-seize raids on lone women drivers are on the increase. Some opportunists strike at random and there's no way of knowing if the pedestrian on the path is safe or not. Most drivers take no notice of pedestrians on the footpath, so when something like this does happen it's sudden and can't be checked in any way. Most women drive with their doors locked, which is the best way to counteract an opportunist opening the door, but the new mode of gaining entry to such a vehicle is by the window being smashed.

There's a way to counteract this, legally, and that's to have the side windows laminated and to carry a can of fluorescent red or green paint. Guess what you do with the paint? Although there were quite a few ads in the YP (not young prisoner, Yellow Pages) advising of window laminating, in reality when these companies were called they gave excuses, blah, blah, blah. Contact one of the national companies; they'll do it and guarantee the job.

The update on this type of vehicle-related crime is that women are being selected and followed! Once selected, the gang then follows their prey and, once stopped at a set of traffic lights or a road junction, they strike, wham, bam, thank you, ma'am.

As for locking the doors on a vehicle when you're in it, you have to decide whether, if an accident should occur, it would hinder help if the emergency services needed to get in. This sort of crime isn't going to go away overnight, but no self-respecting criminal would do such a thing, so my advice would be to take a course in evasive driving techniques and if that doesn't work then you only have one choice – mow the suckers down. What court would convict a lone woman driver of such a thing? Well, maybe that woman who killed her boyfriend and blamed road-rage killers when it was her all along that stabbed him – maybe she wouldn't get off with it.

The police can advise lawful actions, but if your life

is being threatened then you have a right to use the minimum force necessary to escape. In my opinion, that means driving away regardless of what's going on around you – it's your life.

The police advise you, if you're a woman, to drive to a busy place if you suspect you're being followed; drive to a garage forecourt. If you're in heavy traffic, leave a gap between your vehicle and the one in front so you don't get hemmed in, and make mental notes of the descriptions of suspicious-looking characters. God, what a carry-on being a woman. I thought having periods, babies and the change of life sounded bad enough, now this on top of all that. Don't forget, that can of paint can act as a marker on an assailant's boat race or clothing!

So next time you start growling at a lady driver, try and remember that you've got a mother or had a mother; maybe you've got a lady at home and she believes you'd never do such a thing – so behave yourself, leave that sort of thing to the big masculine gorillas.

Ending this chapter on a lighter note, one of the best legal representatives you could ever ask to have on your team, 'Mr T' (short for Tahir Khan), has had his car tampered with! 'T', as his clients know him, discovered that his car had been fitted with a tracking device. It's thought the device was fitted after he'd parked near to the prison of one of his high-profile clients. How was it found? Ah, that would be telling. T is now so feared by his numerous opponents because of his skill at winning cases that they may have started to use these tactics. Anyone who is lucky enough to have Mr T on his or her team is a winner. I can say he's one of a kind, a man for all seasons.

CHAPTER FIVE

CRUISIN' FOR A BRUISIN'

WE'VE ALL GOT one thing in common – we're all different. I hear that Sunderland University in the north of England is to get a grant of £325,000 to help them study the correlation between masculinity and men. I'll do that here and now and they can post the cheque right on to me. I mean, how can you justify that sort of money going in to such research? What about crime and masculinity, isn't it the same as masculinity and men?

What isn't acknowledged very often is that most crime is committed by the age group 13–19 – the teen years. I'll give you a few scenarios of what I mean. Plate glass is shattered as a car is driven straight through the flimsy doors of an electrical retailer's shop. Young men, wearing balaclava SAS masks, jump out and load up the car with luxury electrical goods, and within three minutes they reverse off into the night. The goods are shared out and the group disperses.

In the next chapter, the whole ramraid process is covered in intimate detail, so break open a bottle of the finest, light a few candles, turn down the lights, put some romantic music on and settle down to the thrill of your life, 'cos we're goin' fucking graftin'. Richard 'Faggo' Dodd reveals all – how the raids were planned and what went on behind the scenes. Another gang member – who has chosen to remain anonymous – gives an account of what it was like on one of the raids; how they nicked top-of-the-range whale-tale Cosworths and Cosworth Flips and Golf GTis, regardless of whether they had the biggest locks in the world fitted to their gear sticks.

But for the moment let's push on with this chapter. No peeping into the next one now! Somewhere the squeal of tyres can be heard as a stolen car is being given the handbrake-turn treatment in front of an applauding crowd of onlookers. A show put on for the car-stealing fraternity, sort of 'An Audience With ...' Then we've got a stolen car being driven around just for the sake of a cheap thrill. A police car gives chase, but nothing, nothing is gonna catch this car.

Suddenly an accident and two men die as a result of their masculinity taking over. Looting takes place, the crowd screams for the blood of the police, who are blamed for the deaths of these two young men; their patrol car is taken away – under wraps. No one gets to see if it had, as many had claimed, damage sustained from ramming the stolen car. This book is dedicated to Colin and Dale, the two young men who lost their lives in that crash.

In some way we are not able to grasp the events surrounding such deaths. Was it unemployment, police harassment, lack of amenities, being cut off from society, lack of discipline, being bored with their lot, nastiness? All these subjects were explored and covered. Money was pledged for urban regeneration, European funding, government money was pledged, etc. What, though, was conspicuous by its absence in items commented on was the fact that these instinctive shows of machismo were all committed by young men.

When we think of ramraiders, we don't conjure up a picture in our mind's eye of young women driving around carrying out such crimes. We don't associate females with joyriding, rioting, ramraiding, pacemaking and racing on public roads, etc. When we hear of a serious car crash involving teenagers, and a loss of life is reported, very rarely is it, if ever, that we think of a female driver being responsible. And very often we are right in thinking it was a male driver, a young male driver at that.

Young males commit most crime. OK, it levels out to about evens on small crime like shoplifting, but crimes of violence and sexual crimes are, almost, a male-dominated area. Even as we move higher up the ladder and into the government, local or national, crimes against the state are invariably committed by men. Lord Lucan is a prime example of crime being committed by those in our higher echelons. Doctors are just as bad and usually it is the male of the species that carries out great acts of atrocity – Dr Harold Shipman, remember him?

How many women throughout history have been held responsible for great acts of atrocity against mankind? Difficult to think of many if any, isn't it? Look at the male side of that fence and we find people like Idi Amin, the notorious great dictator of Uganda; Saddam Hussein, former Iraqi dictator; Molosovic, for ethnic cleansing; and of course at the top of the list, Adolf Hitler. Which female can we compare to these men? Helen of Troy for her beauty? Joan of Arc for her courage? The Queen of Sheba for her ways in beguiling men with her power of persuasion? The list is endless, but none can compare to the way men have been accepted as the doers of evil.

Why should it be any different just because we deal with the issue of the lesser crime of ramraiding? All of these issues I've just mentioned have one thing in common – masculinity. Very rarely do we come across a case where a female has transgressed the boundaries. OK, we had the Amazon warriors – women warriors –

but did they ever really exist except in the heads of men? Myra Hindley transgressed those boundaries, but she was still doing the bidding of a male, albeit of her own free will, and in the end she was part and parcel of everything that was going on. Very rarely is someone such as Hindley available for us to compare to a man. What about Rose West, a female sexual deviant who was also part and parcel of the crimes she became involved in, was she acting of her own free will, or was she acting under the influence of Fred West?

OK, so we've got one woman, Rosemary West, who stands out from the crowd in terms of having committed such heinous crimes that she will never be released. That is true enough, but for every Hindley there is the equivalent of God knows how many men doing the same thing – Brady, West, Sutcliffe, Sams, Nielsen, Lowe, Bamber, Black and our own real Hannibal Lecter – Bob Mawdsley. Mawdsley was nicknamed 'spoons' after claims that he'd eaten the brains out of a fellow convict's decapitated head. Years in solitary are to blame.

Does that prove my point about masculinity being connected to crime? Strength is another factor to be taken into account, in that men use this to overpower their prey, to help them dictate their terms to those who are weaker and to impress others. Women with bulging biceps and powerful gluteus maximus, a muscular arse, are a turn-off for most men.

Aggression is a must if a male is to succeed, whether it is in the boardroom or behind the wheel of a stolen car. Controlled aggression, powered by testosterone, can help men achieve their desires in life. How many times have you seen little Johnny being pushed forward by his mother? 'Go on, Johnny, don't let the others get it all, go and get some,' etc. From day one, most males are urged to apply their aggression to such a situation. Look at how sportsmen keep mixing up their emotions off the field of play.

Collymore, former UK soccer player, is a prime example in that he behaved like a warrior on the field, but he couldn't seem to keep it in check when the game ends. And consequently he ended up in all sorts of bother, from bashing up a girlfriend to causing mayhem when out on the town. His aggression on the field was controlled, but off the field it seemed to run wild; his masculinity took over.

Ramraiders suffered the same sort of behavioural patterns in that they were focused, self-disciplined and self-confident during ramraids. When away from this sort of activity, though, some of them steered their lives towards ruin by throwing caution to the wind. The values held by these young men fitted in neatly with the crime of ramraiding – each was competitive, independent and aggressive.

These ramraiders were united by this common bond of masculinity that manifested itself in the form of predatory aggression (big fuck-off words today – too much aggression). Far too often the circumstances leading up to young men going off the straight-and-narrow path is laid squarely at the door of poverty, boredom, inner-city decay, loss of self-esteem and the like.

But if we look at it in terms that violent behaviour amongst young men is normal, then maybe we can begin to understand what it is that is responsible for what is considered abnormal behaviour. As I've said, these ramraiders were united and brought together by virtue of their masculine values; well, in so many words I've said that. The first to spot this sort of thing about male violent behaviour were females. Well, what did you expect me to write? I have to give them credit for spotting this connection and seeing it as part of a continuum of violence uniting individual men and society as a whole.

Masculine rituals such as street racing (cars), challenging others to a fight, joyriding and taking risks are all part of testing themselves against themselves – man pitted against man. Male sexuality extends itself in the form of these rituals; always somewhere along the lines is the mandatory crowd of female groupies, jockeying for position to be the top dog's partner. These sorts of rituals sort the men from the boys and soon a sort of pecking order is established and a leader will emerge.

Ramraiding is the perfect incarnation of a whole range of masculine rituals: risk taking, confidence testing and rising up through the ranks to become a leader – sounds like a game politicians should play! 'Excitement' is also a key word to take into consideration. Remember your first time on a swing? Wow! The world looked a small place from your vantage point high up on that swing – or so it seemed. Then we needed more stimulation; the travelling shows came into town and we progressed to new heights. This sort of thrill was a responsible way of stimulating our senses, but mankind isn't a responsible lot. 'Irresponsibility' is written through us like 'Blackpool' is written all the way through a stick of rock.

Taking risks is seen as a male-dominated quirk, being irresponsible is usually associated with young, and sometimes old, males. (Let's leave single mothers out of this for a moment, although they are a product of irresponsible males.) Death and destruction is courted from the inside of a ramraider's vehicle – machismo at its most potent. The thrills, the spills and the 'fun' of young men testing their mettle – masculinity and crime joining as one.

Mere mortals being propelled into immortality by virtue of a mortal's invention from the 20th century – the car! Immortality being achieved with the help of the car by carrying out the notorious acts of ramraiding en masse. The constraint of normal living being thrown away as they propel themselves into, what seems, oblivion. To be able to transgress the normal everyday constraints applied by their fellow man sets them apart in this death-or-glory task of smashing their way through brick walls or plate-glass doors. Throwing away their self-preservation society certificates and fulfilling their lust for a higher level of thrills and spills once offered by the travelling shows, but long past their sell-by date in satisfying needs.

The harmful way that these men sought to fulfil their lust for excitement was in stark comparison to how others would try to secure such highs from within the boundaries of modern-day laws. Motor sport throws up many a hero; Fangio, Moss, Senna and Damon Hill, like his late father Graham, have all achieved immortal status by legal means, but by demonstrating no less of an aggressive streak necessary to lift them into the realms of being remembered as 'legends'. So did these ramraiders, albeit illegally.

Man's quest to transcend 'mortal' status comes in many forms, from serial murder to writing prose. All are listed for posterity, either to applaud or to show reason why we must not allow such actions. So the ramraiders decided to take the notorious path as opposed to the glorious path. Some of the ramraiders undoubtedly would have made it into such illustrious realms of the SAS or SBS, such were their daring and skill.

Can we compare the likes of Ali to, say, Einstein? One became heavyweight champ of the world in the art of boxing while the other one expounded his theory of relativity. How can one be compared to the other? Difficult, yet each is an act of masculinity, in the sense that each one was competitive in his own discipline. Both of these people had one thing in common – the masculine lust for public glory, acclaim and fame.

Whether one was brought up in a working-class environment, such as that in which the ramraiders were brought up, or with a silver spoon in one's mouth, it mattered not. Each class of upbringing imprinted a certain dogma to reach the top one way or another. Pen pushing or lifting big fuck-off weights – what was the difference? Each class coveted success, spurred on by their masculine values. Whether middle class or working class the desires are the same, but are manifestly different in how they're expressed.

Comparing the goals of working-class lads to their counterparts in the middle-class structure of society, it's plain to see that the only way of masculine expression for the working-class lads is generally by the possession of some sort of physical prowess. Regardless of this physical adeptness, it's not going to get them into the leagues of a generational handover of the reigns of power; by that I mean it's not likely that they'll be taking up a seat in the House of Lords.

They know that, so what other way can they express their masculinity?

We often hear or read of someone from a disadvantaged background making it big, breaking new territory, standing out from the crowd, and for that reason there's much more romanticism attached to such a feat. Most heavyweight boxers have disadvantaged backgrounds; we accept that as a normal trait in that they've fought their way out of the ghetto. Yet we still cling to the rags-to-riches story more so than someone, say, who wins a gold medal for yachting in the Olympics. We accept that such people and the horsy brigade are born into such things, so all the more do we cheer the disadvantaged heavyweight champ.

Such disadvantage and lack of opportunities plays a role in heightening the salience of certain forms of manliness – chromosomes and natural aptitude do not play an important role in the rise to fame and fortune. The ramraider is just as likely to succeed if born into a different class. 'Bollocks!' I hear you say. You read of the things these hooray Henrys get up to it in the officers' club, look at the rituals they have to go through while at public school. Prince Charles went through certain rituals that are considered quite acceptable by the house masters at Eton, etc. We'd be suing the Education Authority if such acts were allowed in state-run schools; shouts of 'bully' and so on would be heard a mile off.

Reduced opportunities can heighten the masculine urge and that's something that no one has really looked at or taken into account. The judge that sits in the Crown Court will have his or her pet hobby; maybe it's hunting – a real bloodthirsty sport if ever there was one. I never see queues of people sabotaging ramraids like I saw hunt saboteurs trying to spoil an afternoon's chase.

Seeking out your own identity is somewhat fashionable. We get this notion from the odd characters we see around us, or so I say, if they can make it then so can we. They, who have made it, might use a gimmick to advance them along the squares of life – do we do likewise? Why, then, do we look upon such acts as ramraiding as being less than odd or being different?

These young men were the trendsetters of their time; they led and others followed. It was a natural step for those that looked on. They were witnessing something new, a phenomenon! Many young men followed suit and took up this fashionable crime as a way of expressing, developing and reinforcing their masculine side. They identified with what was going on and were going to acquire a new identity for themselves; an 'I'm having some of that' attitude.

This was their version of masculinity, while others would emulate famous footballers, cricketers, etc. An example was set and it was to be followed or even bettered. Of course, acquiring masculine values was fraught with dangers; we'll look at that later when we delve into the criminal trial of one particular ramraid gang.

Maybe you can see what I'm getting at here. Surely you have a sneaky admiration for some of these ramraiders by now? Surely you can, to some extent, see what this chapter is leading up to? It leads up to the ramraiders carrying out highly daring raids in a very organised manner. I don't intend to give excuses as to why they did it, or even to glamorise their initiative, but certainly I can't help having a romantic notion that the north-east of England had a love affair with ramraiding.

Yes, I know we're going to get the realists coming out of the closet and laying down the law, telling us about the damage to other people's lives caused as a direct result of the ramraiders' gall. I accept that and so did they when they received some very big prison sentences, so I've saved you putting pen to paper, although still write as you're one of my readers so I respect what you've got to say. Mind you, that doesn't mean I have to listen to it.

It might seem that the ramraid gangs were on a path of self-destruction and never even stood a cat in hell's chance of ever getting away with it. On the contrary, they were very successful and such was the skill of the drivers that they were unlikely to be caught in a police chase, unless of course the police helicopter was out and about, but there was a way they dealt with that, a very clever way. These ramraiders were a clever lot and win the prize for ingenuity in running their own covert surveillance operation on the police helicopter – more of that later.

These ramraid gangs were brought up by a society of manual workers, so naturally their skills would lean in the direction of manual skills. Hand and eye co-ordination was going to come in handy for helping with their driving techniques.

The rites of passage having been accomplished, it put the ramraiders on a different level to the ordinary guy in the street. Masculine values were picked up from their peers and since their peers had complex emotional lives it was easy to opt for the rich pickings that a ramraider's life would bring them. Yeah, those streets were soon gonna be paved with gold, well … err, sort of. Electrical goods and the like were the gold of the ramraiders.

The identities now acquired were to be sustained – until they were caught, and some, eventually, were broken down by the system and became junkies, lost in their despair at failing in their profession. The cracks that were already there within their personalities had now been widened by the wedge of the prison system – loss of liberty could do what nature wouldn't have done.

The slang used to depict male vehicle crime gives off a masculine aroma by the mere use of words 'ram', 'hotrodding', 'joyriding', 'shafted' and other words that conjure up sexual notions. The face of public disapproval was overshadowed by the romance attached to such daring raids; the cheek of gangs stripping premises bare, and the brazenness of them doing so while security guards stood like impotent pieces of flesh, drew gasps and nods of approval from their supporters.

For those of you that can drive, haven't you ever had a buzz, a high, from driving at speed? Maybe a hot summer's day, the windows down, the rush of wind, the gleam of the sun on the road, you're wearing shades, looking cool and feeling like a million dollars, yes? Now, if that's so then you can imagine what a ramraider must feel surging through his veins when he's doing something far superior to this; the buzz, the high, the rush and all of the adrenaline on top of that! Can't you admire them? In some way, maybe the closest you've ever come to that is to kick a ball around a park, catch a few fish, climb a tree, steal some apples out of a garden, or maybe sneak into a nightclub when you were 17.

Male-orientated crime is somewhat unacceptable when carried out by females! What is acceptable for males is often not acceptable to society for females to partake of. It would seem that certain types of crime have the word 'man' stamped all over them and are strictly taboo for females. The courts come down heavy on female lawbreakers and, with this in mind, it shows the hypocrisy of the system. It also shows that the lawmakers have their own masculine views on this score. If we look at it from that point of view, it supports what I've given over to you.

In fact, such crimes as ramraiding are expected to be carried out by young males. Society accepts that. Can you imagine if a gang of ramraiders turned out to be an all-female gang? The media would have a field day, and a picnic besides, reporting on such matters! There'd be profiles on each one of them, a full background status report. Yet an all-male gang would have the usual write-ups we've come to expect – brought up in a working-class environment, from an area of high unemployment and with little prospect of finding a way out of it all.

White collar crime is just as acceptable – look at what goes on in the stock market. We've come to accept that white-collar crime is part and parcel of life, we are equally tolerant of working-class crime – each to their own.

You wouldn't park your car in an unlit car park with weeds growing out of the cracks in the tarmac at night-time. You've come to look out for the signs and that's the same of crime and masculinity. The minute some people see shipyards and the like they seem to go into 'I'm the hardest bastard in town' mode. The environment can cause changes within all of us, so shouldn't we take into account the areas these ramraiders hail from?

Masculinity shows itself more so in the 'street' environment than anywhere, other than a gym or boxing club. OK, you might disagree, you know what I mean though. Look at the average household. Who is it that has to make the money stretch, do the chores and maybe even hold down a full-time job? It's usually a woman. The male might have long gone or taken it on himself to do other things of interest and to his own benefit; he might have his hobby and because of that he expects his partner to do all the other things needed to keep a household running. During that time, where are the children?

Kids are streetwise, kids from a working-class environment that is. Young men forming their own cliques and sub-groups make for the streets, as if magnetised by some unseen power drawing them to the centre of attraction. During the daytime, such places would hold no attraction for streetwise teenagers. I mean, who wants to be in the midst of women doing their shopping and the coming and going of daytime society?

School comes to an end and teatime has arrived. 'Thank fuck for that,' little Jimmy says. Working-class youths start gathering and calling out for each other, as if in some mighty jungle – an urban concrete jungle. Street gangs are a breeding ground for hoodlums; unknown to their parents, they seek out the joys and pain of growing up on a street corner. I, of course, refer only to those that seek out such a life; there are many respectable and well-brought-up teenagers, and I wouldn't disagree with what their parents say about how they've brought up their children in spite of what goes on around them.

But for those that have sought out a different life, they're the ones that must accept some responsibility for the way their life has gone. Street corners are a place for hanging around and are off limits for those that seek out a quieter life. Streets become a place best avoided by women. The threat of intimidation sees all but the strongest willing to set foot in such places. I could name these areas, but I don't want to be accused of favouritism amongst the streetwise fraternity. Car thieves, joyriders and ramraiders all sprung from such street colleges.

Male harassment, intimidation and violence is often directed towards women and also towards those that don't conform to their masculine ways. It's not the sort of place you'd walk along shouting, 'I'm gay!' 'Queer bashing' represents heterosexual dominance and reinforces masculinity; even if some are closet gays themselves, they dare not show it. White-collar workers wouldn't walk down a street past a teenage gang for fear of violence, yet a working-class car mechanic might not give a second thought to such things; he's accustomed to it, maybe even used to be one himself.

How often have you heard of a gang of youths attacking some respectable law-abiding citizen out to stop them vandalising the community? That sort of thing goes on around us all the time; a group of 16-year-olds attack a middle-class man for coming out of his house and telling them to be quiet, they kill him and run for it, they get caught and only one is charged with a serious offence, he pleads a rough upbringing. You know, the usual stuff, he was unloved, shifted from pillar to post, he was coming off drugs after being addicted, he was brought up by a single parent, blah, blah. He gets three years and lives happily ever after.

Such a scenario seems to be acceptable to those in the judiciary. Maybe if it happened to them they'd change their minds, but since they drive or are driven everywhere they don't have to suffer such a thing happening to them by virtue of setting their foot on a working-class pavement. Street corners can be an exciting place to be, exchanging stories of who's locked up, what's new and what's to be done – sort of a conference centre. Would any Crown Court judge relish the thought of walking through the middle of such a gang while they were in conference? Would they fuck, like.

What people forget, though, is that many years ago the street corners were also packed with out-of-work adults. Social intercourse was common; talking that is, not shagging in the streets – trust you lot to think of that. As the social structure changed over the years, the streets were left to the younger and rougher person, and to the police. Oh yes, the police existed and do play some small role in this book.

Poorly educated, unqualified and unemployed young males make up the typical street gang and yet they seem to develop their own unique way of interacting with each other. Buying and selling social intercourse has changed into buying and selling drugs. Physical presence means everything and by that I mean toughness and strength. Joyriding is also seen as a toughness; being accepted as the best car thief in the area can be an accolade from one group, but from another group – the police – it can be seen as a means to end your time on the street: one way or another!

Ramraiding and car thieving go hand in hand and the police are often used as a test; luring the police into ambushes might well be the testing ground for trainees. By pitting themselves against such opposition and by taunting the police to chase them, they can see how far they can push themselves. Aggression is vented against the police from the safety of a balcony or the window of a derelict building, a hail of stones raining down on their foe. Policing the working-class city brings many of these traps, but such incidents are now a rare thing, although they still happen from time to time.

So it would seem that the training grounds for ramraiding have come from a background of street culture and clashes with danger of some sort. We'll find out if that's true in the next chapter when we get to hear it straight from the horse's mouth.

Rioting became a way of life for these ramraiders. You've only got to examine the history of rioting to find out that rioting and crime associated with rioting, such as looting, are part and parcel of the same thing, cause and effect and all that jazz that criminologists use. Speaking of criminologists, what a load of bollocks they come out with, and the thing is, are any of them man enough to be able to give a solution to it all? It would take a masculine criminologist to take the bull by the horns.

With the sort of life on offer in the street-corner environment, it's plain to see why these delinquent teenagers become hoodlums. What's there for them? What's on offer? A bit of window shopping and a bit of ramraiding here and there. What can match the emotional charge on offer to them? Stuck between the choice of having to draw the dole every week or turn to a bit of crime to supplement their income, what could they do?

Identifying such a group of renegade teenagers from

the young men at large in a working-class city isn't too difficult. Each bears an aggressive tough masculinity, worn like a badge of honour, like the patches of a Hell's Angel gang member. Crime, men and masculinity go well together and I think I've earned that £325,000 grant – saved them a job, I have. It will only tell us what we already know. How can such research come up with anything else?

Learning the car-theft trade is an easy one, but only those with quick wits about them will survive. Skills are handed down, new methods are soon picked up and, with all those cars to choose from, what can get in their way?

I'm going to spoon feed you some facts – yes, I'm on one of my missions again! – to show you how certain areas are more crime ridden and less likely to vote against their working-class roots than others. Here's something for you to take on board. Guess which areas within the boundaries of England, Scotland and Wales have the highest percentage of occupants on government benefits? No need to guess, I'll tell you. The answer is below. Now, before you take a peep I can tell you that the areas are all considered as being Labour Party safe-seat areas. Which means they get fuck-all off the Conservatives and since Labour consider the areas safe as houses they get fuck-all from them either – our run-down areas just can't win, can they? Here's the answer based on end-of-millennium figures:

NORTH-EAST of ENGLAND	24%
WALES	23%
NORTH-WEST (Manchester)	22%
SCOTLAND	21%
HUMBERSIDE	19%

We have to hold both Labour and Conservative parties responsible for gross neglect to the above areas. Compare that to the figures below showing a contrast in the way these areas were considered to be Conservative safe-seat areas:

SOUTH-EAST of ENGLAND	11%
EAST of ENGLAND	12%
SOUTH-WEST of ENGLAND	14%
EAST MIDLANDS	15%
WEST MIDLANDS	17%

No wonder house prices are flourishing down south; they can afford to pay for the fuckers. My pal, Dave Courtney, has a house in London worth about £500,000; he's got a great big mural painted on the side of it. It's Dave doing what looks to be a ramraid on horseback; well, it looks that way, like a knight with a giant lance charging.

Dave says the mural's on the side of the house so that the rookie policemen can find it easier when they want to raid it; in fact, at one point he left the key to his front door behind the desk of his local police station so as to save them kicking his front door in. But I digress, if you want to read more on Dave then pick up his book *Stop the Ride, I Want to Get Off,* or check out the website of crimebiz.com.

You'll have noticed that the figures I've thrown up reflect certain areas' connections with crime. I mean, look at poor Wales, always at the back of the queue when handouts are on the go. There should be one big motorway from North Wales to South Wales, give the people a decent road; maybe then people will plough money into the area, which is full of jobless men. Scotland, build a giant motorway all the way through it from north to south and, while we're on it, improve the A66 and the A1, all death spots in northern England.

I mentioned some while ago, in 1998, that Sean Connery (007) was turned down for a knighthood due to his contacts with the Scottish Socialist Party, but if he got into power then maybe he'd be able to sort it! Fuck me, didn't the government go and give him his knighthood the following year? So maybe now we'll see some decent roads Up North.

Another matter is the way the Labour government acted on car-tax dodgers. Have you seen what they did to tax (Excise Duty, they call it) evaders' cars? They pick them up off the roadside and crush them into little squares. You can't tell me the government can condemn organised crime groups that go around with menaces demanding money; these are the same sort of strong-arm tactics: 'Pay up or we'll fuck your car up, mate!' Ramraiders didn't give a fuck if their car was taxed or not.

The north-east of England has one of the worst crime records in the country according to a report produced by Autoglass. They know this because by looking at their figures they can see traits running through certain areas. The city of Newcastle and the town of Gateshead had the worst records for 'smash & grab' car crime.

Twenty cities and towns were assessed and Newcastle beat places like Glasgow and Liverpool. When you consider that a little over a quarter of Autoglass's customers in the Newcastle area reported such incidents to the police, we are only seeing the tip of the iceberg! The lack of confidence in the police being able to catch the perpetrators of such vandalism is reflected in these figures.

Northumbria Police Force insist that crime has fallen and point out figures that would indicate theft from cars had fallen by 13.1 per cent during the last year of the old millennium – which means, if what Autoglass say is true about only 25 per cent of car-crime victims reporting such incidents, the figures produced by the police would support the information included in Autoglass's report.

I wonder who it is that scores for all the lolly from doing these reports; please don't say 'criminologists', please, no! They're all a load of plonkers; I haven't come across one yet that can speak for the people. I had another plonker from one of the universities down souf; I asked him if he could help out on another unrelated matter. Fuck-all came back from my three letters. Then out of the blue he writes and asks for a Charlie Bronson book (*Silent Scream*); you can guess what the answer was!

Wild and young – Teenagers in Britain are considered to be at greater risk of wrecking their lives than anywhere else in Europe, according to a shock report by the Home Office action team. The report warns of massive problems ahead unless government ministers take action now. The report showed that 60 per cent of 15-year-olds had been drunk at least twice and that 10 per cent of men aged between 18 and 24 were alcoholics!

Compared to the rest of Europe, teenagers in Britain were said to take more drugs and drink more, and girls are more likely to become pregnant. Unemployment amongst youths in the EU was above average and levels of literacy below the rest of the industrialised world. For £50,000 I could have told them that. Don't these people read any of my books?

The report went on to say that 11 per cent of 11–15-year-olds are regular smokers and 15–16-year-olds took more drugs than any other EU country. Teenage pregnancies occur twice as much in Britain as in Germany, are three times higher than in Italy and are six times higher than in Holland. Education standards, according to the report, are the worst in Europe. Just out of interest, I wrote a book many years ago called *Teenagers and their Problems*. It's probably out of print now, but it said it all in there. The report finally called for a cabinet minister to be appointed for youths and to tackle youth problems.

When you read the following chapter you'll find that Faggo explains how ramraiding started – joyriding. Intervention by some sort of minister would have to be on level terms; by that I mean a very young minister would have to be appointed, someone under the age of 25. I mean, what's the point of having someone as old as the hills unless it's someone who's firmly in touch with the needs of such a targeted age group? How's about an ex-criminal made good – Dave Courtney?

Below is an update on the car-crime capital (England, Scotland and Wales) from a more recent report this side of the new millennium. Here's a list of the top five based on an Autoglass report:

No. 1: Birmingham
No. 2: Manchester
No. 3: Newcastle upon Tyne & Gateshead
No. 4: Glasgow
No. 5: Cardiff

The table excludes the area within the M25 and the worst places outside of London. To top it all, they reckon a vehicle is attacked every 23 seconds. What isn't highlighted or even mentioned in these two reports I've quoted from is what makes people turn to such crime. In a nutshell, there is a word that encapsulates it – 'boredom'. Young thugs have plenty of free time on their hands and are cruisin' for a bruisin'.

I'll give you an example of what I mean. Residents living on a run-down council estate in Chester-le-Street, County Durham have suffered lack of amenities for many years. The boredom threshold among the local youths has been surpassed many a time. The Avenues Estate is so run down that even the Rottweilers go around in pairs, unemployment is the norm, drug dealing, prostitution and other criminal activities are rife.

During a nightly cruise around the area, little by way of a police presence was seen, the supposed community work run by volunteers was not to be seen, the council's supposed 'pulling out of all the stops' was not seen in what they claim to be help for local youngsters. Boredom was the key word; we were even bored driving around the place, a rat run and maze of little streets, many boarded up and visibly run down.

So it was of no surprise when a few nights later a car was driven into a house as the family slept in the early hours. Once awakened they felt forced to flee.

The car was stolen, driven by joyriders – bored joyriders. For such a close-knit area to become victim to such an attack, it surely indicates that the council hasn't looked fully at all options.

I'm not saying that these joyriders are little cherubs and deserve a few hundred grand spent on improving facilities as, after all, someone owned the car that was concertina'd into the wall. The car owner, the occupants of the house and the joyriders were all victims in one way or another and, for that matter, we might as well say that funds should be available for all of them. Money, though, isn't always the answer.

I can tell you that I once had an argument with a police officer. It was pissing down. I was walking my dog across a field and he, the policeman, walked some hundred metres to get to where I was. He had been sitting in a white Transit van and I recognised him as 'Freddie' (he's mentioned in the next chapter).

He was shouting his head off that if my dog crapped then it, the mess, would have to be cleaned up. He poked his garlic-flavoured face right into mine. He'd invaded my three-foot barrier. There was only him and me, nothing to stop me poking him in the eye and telling him to stop invading my space. The rain was dripping off the end of his nose. He'd taken all that effort out of himself to tell me something I already knew. His eyes were bulging, his breath was blowing on my face and he needed a shave.

He was going on about some cochlea strain of worm that could blind children, which I was fully aware of (if the dog has worms and messes on a playing field and young children get the muck in their eye, it can eventually blind them, but my dog was fully wormed and had all of the inoculations that any decent dog-owner would have made sure of).

Anyway, I let him prattle on and on. He stopped and I pushed my face within three inches of his and started my barking! When I bark I can make one hell of a noise, and he could see he'd annoyed me. And since he'd used such a tactic on me, he deserved some of his own medicine. I mean, you wouldn't go up to someone who hadn't committed a misdemeanour and start shouting and bawling at them square on – he did.

I wasn't some young 'un he could throw his weight about with. I gave him short shrift and asked him what he was doing for the community. 'What do you mean, this lot around here? I wouldn't do fuck-all for them!' I asked him why he didn't put some of his spare time into the local Mafioso gangs of kids; maybe even buy a football for a game on a Saturday afternoon. 'I wouldn't part with my piss to this lot around here,' was his reply. So there you have the problem; too many frustrations for local police officers. Maybe he hadn't had his leg over the previous night, who knows?

But what I can tell you is that a few months later a local hoodlum organised a football match between the local Mafioso gang and the local police. The game was held on a Saturday morning and, although it was part organised by a Special Constable, it brought some newspaper interest. The hoodlums won, but on that day the local bobby won some respect. But guess what? He wasn't ever seen on the beat in that area again! Can you believe such a story? It really happened – I was there!

So you see, that's what's needed, a back-to-basics approach, a bobby on the beat building up a rapport with the locals. Oh, Freddie – he fucked off over the field with his tail between his legs and I swear I saw him put his foot in a pile of dog dirt as he stormed off to his 'White Van Man' van. Poetic justice really.

An incident that happened in April of 2000 lends credibility to the above story. A 12-year-old boy from North Tyneside rammed the side of a house with a steamroller. The screams of the lady of the house alerted her husband and son to the situation, and the family had to be evacuated after the house was declared unsafe. The young lad was charged with motoring offences, a 12-year-old boy charged with motoring offences – unreal, isn't it, what are they going to do, ban him for the next five years until he gets his licence at the age of 17? The charge of aggravated vehicle taking will set this lad on the merry-go-round of the legal system and God knows how he'll end up.

We've all done foolish pranks as kids – haven't we? Sometimes a prank can end up far more serious than we intend; OK, a steamroller through the side of a house is a bit of a stupid prank, but if this lad was occupied with other things maybe this wouldn't have happened!

CHAPTER SIX

GRAFTING

'GRAFTING', FOR THOSE of you not in the know, is a terminology used by the criminal fraternity – going to work, doing the business, etc. Richard Thomas Dodd AKA Faggo was one of the brains behind a £3½ million ramraid spree, albeit in the sense that he only conspired to carry out such acts.

When reading this you have to bear in mind he was so slippery that he could only be pinned down to conspiring with others to do such acts. Since Faggo has not actually been convicted of carrying out such acts it would be wrong of anyone to put him in the frame – he could be recharged with certain offences he was seen to admit to.

Once acquitted of an offence under the old law, you could not be retried for that offence. OK, we're bound to get some fucking know-all coming out of the woodwork with some sort of example to disprove such things, but in general you get the message.

Well, if I was tell you that Faggo wasn't acquitted of anything, that he pleaded guilty to the 'conspiracy' bit only after he was two weeks into his trial ... He seemed badgered into making such a decision; in my opinion the prosecution didn't stand a cat in hell's chance of securing a conviction for what they sought. Faggo stood his ground and was going 'not guilty' all the way. Anyway, more of that trial later on, I don't want to spoil your fun of listening (reading) to what Faggo and another party has to tell you in this chapter. The contents of what follow are the contributions from Faggo and a party that wishes to remain anonymous.

Remember that the gang Faggo was part of was attributed with £3$^{1}/_{2}$ million worth of damage and property theft. Over to you, Faggo & Co:
Faggo: I've been called Faggo for as long as I can remember. It started out with me being caught smoking, I think it was a Woodbine. I was made to chew it and from then on I was called 'Fag' and if I was asked to go anywhere it was 'Fag go ...' and so it became 'Faggo'.

My first real memory of wanting to be involved with motorbikes and other fast stuff was riding a BMX bicycle and doing wheelies on it. You had that lot who wanted to do stunts such as bunny hopping and the like, but for me it was pure scorch-the-rubber stuff; fuck that other easy stuff, that was for the limp-wrist brigade.

The natural progression from the BMX was to a motorbike, something powerful, and by that I don't mean a Honda Goldwing or some other old man's bike. For me it was the faster two-stroke engines, much more zippy, plenty of red banding, lots of torque and high revs made them go like stink. The bigger the two-stroke engine the better it would go, and some people say great for using in robbery situations, not that I've had any convictions for such things. Mind you, I've had plenty of filth try to knock me off my bike. To them it was all a game. If I'd lost my legs they wouldn't have given a toss, but the police told me that I was the best they'd come across.

Loads of the coppers didn't care if I was going to be captured for anything, they just wanted to catch me. There I was, a moving target, me on two wheels, them on four: cruisers, Cosworths, none could catch me, but I'd still end up being banned from driving – cunts. Anonymous: I'd plan lots of ramraids with the other gang members, which is all right to say as we've all been nicked and served time because of it. The cars that had to be used were hoisty motors. The gang would go on the hunt for them until they seen a car they wanted, but that wasn't my speciality so I'll hand you over to my mate Faggo.

Faggo: Aye, we'd go into an area and scour around on the lookout for something nice and we'd just take it. How we got it depended on what the locks were like. We've even used a Stihl motovised saw to cut gear locks off. We didn't fuck about with stuff like slide hammers for that type of lock. What we'd do is this: we'd have to go and get the stihl saw; we'd have it started up in our car 'cos we didn't want it letting us down when we needed it – what's the point of getting there and trying to fire it up from cold? A few seconds of sparks and smoke and we'd have the fucker off, then we'd be off, away with it.

We'd go to the coast, look around hotels. 'COSY!' somebody would shout and we'd all give it the once over. We'd mainly target the Metro Centre; you'd be sure to end up with a set of wheels in A1 condition. Piss easy to take from these places; full of cars and nobody watching over them, they were mugging the shopper off just as much as we were.

If we'd see a car we liked and it needed the Stihl saw treatment, we'd just blatantly take it in broad daylight. We wouldn't even be masked up, but not during the day. There'd be smoke and sparks flying out of the car. The noise coming from the engine of this saw sounded like we were revving a scrambler up inside the car; we couldn't have heard a police siren even if we wanted to. Not that it would've made much of a difference.

We'd nick all sorts of turbo cars and flog them to the ramraid gangs for a ton [£100]. The favourite was the Sierra Sapphire Cosworth or the Cosworth Flip, which was the three-door one, Porsche 944 Turbos, anything quick, anything that would do over 150mph we'd get. Sixteen-valvers like the Golf Gti or an Astra 16-valve – anything 16-valvish, anything turboish, that's what we'd get. They had to be turbo powered because they were used as the getaway cars and had to run fully loaded.

For ramming, we'd take any old shit. We'd just pull up on the street and it'd be gone, even six o'clock at night. People would be sitting there having their tea and we'd take them, right from under their noses, but we'd wear masks for that – smother [mask] on and take it away.

We used to go through Washington and that and find empty garages, put the car in and put locks on the doors; after all, we didn't want any other cunt coming along and nicking our car, did we? We'd use such places as if they were our own garages; the hardest part, though, was going back to the garage and getting the fucker – that was the naughtiest part. You'd never know if the law were waiting for you – nobody wants to go to the garage, nobody!

As soon as the law found a high-powered car in such a garage they'd leave it there and wait to catch us. They used to sit and watch the garage, so if you went back to the garage loads of them used to pile on you. It's happened to us and we've been fighting the police to get away, and that's just what we had to do. There'd be three or four of us, maybe five with a batman if we were going to do a job on a high-street area.

The batman just stands outside the shop – he's the man with the bat. If anyone pulled up, say, like security guards, then his job was to put their windows out in their cars and whatever and, terrorise them. They weren't meant to cause anyone any harm, but windscreens on security-guards vans and stuff like that, they'd use it on that, like. That was the batman's job really. He'd stand there from start to finish next to the shutters or the wall or whatever till it was done. He was just used to scare people off really, that's all.

When we used to go and collect cars from our lock-ups we didn't carry a bat; it would be in the car ready for the batman to go graft with. We'd even take the seats out of the cars, leaving the driver's seat, just so you could get more stuff in them. We'd also paint the windows black and all that so you could only see out of the windscreen.

We'd plan such raids after we knew the cars were in the garages, five cars on the graft, the more the merrier and it would give you more chance of getting away. The plan was to meet on the Coach Road and to go from there to the place we had lined up, and ram it. We used to meet up long before such a raid was planned; we'd meet up with each other all the time and talk about what we we're going to do.

One of us would say, 'I've seen this brilliant fucking snout [tobacco] pitch to do, let's go and have a look at it.' Another would say, 'All right then, let's go and sort it, we'll go tomorrow during the day and case it.' We wouldn't all be there at such a meeting, we'd be split into cells, but we'd all join up to do the graft.

We'd go during the day to see what the easiest ways in and out were, and the best way back to the garage from there. The more cars that could be organised on the graft, the safer you felt. If somebody was going to get caught then you'd know you were a better driver than them; it's them that's going to get caught, isn't it?

If the pitch looked OK, we'd plan to meet up to do the job, different teams in different cars. Maybe up to five teams would be on standby to do one big job; if there's enough for everybody then everybody goes. Gaffs like these needed to be hit in a big way.

Say the place was a big warehouse, then everybody was ready, but if it was a little perfume place planned or a little snouter, then only one car would be planned for. It all depended on how big the place was and how much was in it. If you knew more than one car would be filled and everybody could fill their cars from the stock, then why not take them all – have a big party? Sometimes two cars would be planned on the graft. there were six of us, that's how many got done, so really three in each car and that's the way it was – the six of us used to meet and talk it over.

The graft would be sussed out and then we'd all be told about it and we'd say, 'What do you reckon?' Four of us would go down to wherever it was, look at the graft, have a talk about it and tell each other what way we'd be going back and all that so you'd know what ways everyone was heading out. The plan was then to phone each other straight away once you'd got home, to make sure you'd all got back safely and just crack on about it if all was to go well.

Smothers were picked up from Army & Navy stores. we didn't plan for any alibis 'cos we didn't plan to be hanging about and, of course, since we'd be using choredy [stolen] cars, we weren't planning on stopping to take a 'producer'. We didn't plan to use any alibis 'cos if you were caught then you were only caught for one job – we'd planned on being sent away for a 12-monther if it came to that. People were just getting six and nine months for them at the time, but we never thought about the conspiracy part of it.

We just thought, if you get caught for one then that's it, and we felt that if we were smothered up and had our turtles [gloves] on then even if the place had cameras they couldn't prove anything. They couldn't come along and say it was you, could they? They couldn't prove nowt – or so we thought. It wasn't until later on that we started thinking 'conspiracy'; we thought everyone was a hundred per cent staunch, sort of thing. We were strong at the time, but everyone just went their own way at the finish, done their own thing, soon as we went to jail that was.

We were known as the Yellow Pages ramraiders because we used to look into it a couple of times to see where a place was. Maybe we'd heard about something and needed to check it out, and there we'd all be looking in the Yellow Pages to see where it was. We never just went into the pages with a dart and said, 'Here, we'll do that.' It was just really to see what was there, tabs, tobacconists and the likes. The first pages we used to turn to were 'Tobacconists' to see where they were located. This was the main factor in deciding if we'd go and look at it. I mean, you wouldn't want to be travelling miles and miles with hoisty snout in the car.

If the place was in the middle of a high street then it wouldn't be avoided just because it was in a busy place. Someone would go into the place in the middle of the day and just wander into a store room, just walk in or something and spy the snout in the corner or watch out for it being delivered, so we'd know the place was going to be worth turning over.

The snout would come in Lynx wagons and Hoover wagons, and people soon cottoned on to them. We'd be driving down this road one day and there was a Lynx wagon or a Hoover wagon and it was full of snout. We all had hard-ons at the sight of it. They were taking it to a shop and we thought, that must be the score. The stupid thing was that the snout was in 5,000 boxes of Regal and all that. Shutters up and that was it, you could see them clear as day screaming to be picked up – by us.

We followed the wagon and found out the storage place. We then checked the Yellow Pages for the name of the place and sure enough it come back as a 'Tobacconist', so we knew we'd struck gold. We'd check out the A–Z map of the area to find out the layout of the roads.

We'd plan for three minutes to get in and out of the place, with a driver in place who'd sometimes be doubling up as a scanner man. He'd have a scanner in his inside pocket and have his earplug in so he'd be able to listen to the police; that was when the police used the old system, now apparently most of their transmissions are encrypted.

The scanner man could be a passenger if need be, but the plan was that there'd be the driver/scanner man, the batman and the rest of the team to handball the stuff out. If it was planned to take two cars and a car to ram, then that would mean the other driver, the rammer, would have to jump into one of the other getaway cars.

Should we have planned to have five different firms on the pitch then it would take only one rammer.

Some firms have started with two on the graft and then another one comes into it and it goes on from there. Our team had six in it. I've seen people go to graft ransack somewhere and there's three of them on the graft, and when they come away there's eight of them in the car. Somebody's told somebody else and they've been waiting there for the place to be rammed and they're then grabbing gear as well and they end up in the car.

A little job wouldn't take much planning; two or three people could rive a shutter off a shop front just by hand. They can manhandle it up; bollards make no difference whatsoever. Three people would just get down and rive it up, just like that. It comes up away from the holders and it pulls it out, leaving it flapping. Behind that there's usually a glass door, and boosh! In it goes, or so they say! They duck in and get in that way.

Their car would still be parked at the front, waiting with its driver. That car can't leave them, and if the driver sees police coming then they have to toot the horn and the others have gotta get back to the car. As soon as the horn toots they know they've gotta get outta there, fucking fast.

A good driver will wait – no matter what. Them that leave, their arses must have went, but like, when you're a driver it's your job to get them away – no matter what. It's an unwritten rule that the driver has to stay; if he nashed and left them then they and all the others wouldn't want you as a driver, would they? You wouldn't be asked to drive any more and you'd probably get a hiding to go with your P45. So if the gang's going to get caught, the driver's gonna be caught with them, that's the way it is.

The way these raids were happening wasn't as complicated as the papers made out; a gang might turn up at a tobacconist with a fast car and maybe a sledgehammer to do the shutter in. They mainly did high-street areas away from the areas occupied by flats and the like. Certain areas were no-go areas as the filth would patrol regularly. A rough area with loads of people living jam-packed on top of each other would have to be looked at differently than an area in a well-to-do place.

Industrial estates were more our cup of tea for planning things. We'd reckon that you'd have at least three to four minutes, but the police started using code areas. It took them a while to cotton on to such an idea; they'd come over the scanner with coded areas, say like, if it was a Newcastle area it would be 'NE ...' and so on. You'd have to find out postal-code areas and plan things that way; we planned for all sorts of things happening.

The crafty filth had different codes for different areas; if something happened then all of the police went to that area. Instead of them saying, 'I'm at the ...'

they'd say, 'I'm at East 10,' or 'North 6', or something like that, so the scanner man was confused as he didn't know if they were coming to your area or not. I mean, if the law caught them then they'd have to ram their way out, but not like you'd think, it wouldn't be foot flat to the floor – no way! You'd end up cattling the radiator or something.

Anonymous: I remember one raid I was on at Jackson Street in Gateshead. We had two cars on the graft, two Cosworths. Right in the middle of Jackson Street there's a little alley and one car left. They tooted the horn, as Freddie had come on top.

He came braying around the corner, three got out of the shop unit and got into the first Cosy with their tabs; they didn't get as many tabs as they'd wanted and they nashed. There was only one car left. Two had come out of the unit to get into that Cosy, but there was still one of the gang left in the unit.

Freddie wouldn't get out of the van, he just sat there. The driver in the Cosy couldn't leave 'cos he didn't have his full crew. One had to jump out of the Cosy and go see what was the matter with the last man who still hadn't come out of the unit. The engine on the Cosy was revving ready to go, the driver had it in gear and his foot was on a spring, ready to let it off and go, but he couldn't – no matter what, he had to wait.

'Howway! What the fuck are you doing, man? The fucking filth's out here!' What had happened was, when we were all in there he'd gone into a stock room, no one'd seen him. We were pulling trolleys around like nobody's business and one of them went across the door and trapped him inside. All the shouting in the world wouldn't get him out.

The trolley was moved. 'That fucking Freddie's out there, the other lot's gone, we've gottafuckoff.' That's how fast we were speaking, but we could all understand each other no matter how fast we talked to each other. It's a trick we learned from the Scottish. Have you ever heard two Glasweigens talking to each other fast? Clever fuckers.

By the time we were all ready to go a few more law cars, cruisers, had turned up. 'Look at them fuckers!' By this time there were about eight law cars there – we were blocked in. 'We'll get through them, they'll bottle it before we do, come on.' Anyone else would have panicked, shit themselves and maybe just wellied it on the throttle. Not our driver, he knew what he was doing. He kept the revs up high but was only driving slow, handbrake up so it was just clutch and throttle. We got closer, closer, and suddenly the law car pulled away! 'Fucking hell, he's letting us out, he's bottled ...' Couldn't hear the rest as we shot out of the street. They mustn't have wanted their cars damaged and rammed.

There were stories going about that ramraiders had smashed police cars up, just cruising around looking for police cars to smash up. Whickham Police Station got it one night. A car pulled into the station and all the firm were balied up. They'd been chased up Swalwell Bank, along Whickham High Street, then they pulled into the police station and started putting all the windows out on the cruisers.

They were using bats and hammers and that, and it came up on the scanner, 'They've got guns, don't approach them, they've got guns.' But when they went outside and they seen all the windows smashed they said, 'No, they've smashed all the cruiser windscreens!' So they came down from there, down Lobley Hill, and flew up Derwentwater Road in Gateshead, and they seen a CID car parked up. They put the window out on that car, blew up to Gateshead Police Station, put cruiser windows out there and worked their way along the Felling [Felling Police Station]. There was a CID car sitting at the gates of Felling compound and they put that window out too. The copper inside was screaming, crying. He was saying, 'They're trying to kill 'es.'

Some of the police were liberty takers; they thought they could get away with bullying people. That's what it was – bullying. They'd just start rajing the young 'uns up; both uniformed and CID police could take things too far. I remember one young 'un called Jiff. He was pulled into the back of a police van. You couldn't see what was going on but you could 'narf hear it and the van was rocking back and forwards.

People were walking past, ignoring what the police were doing. Jiff was only about 16 years old and of average build. He didn't stand a chance.

He was let out of the van and in a hell of a state; a few weeks later he was found dead up in the attic of a friend's house – nothing sinister, just dead. [The author of this book has confirmed this story of Jiff passing away. His full name has been withheld to save any further pain for his family.] Work that one out for yourself! Of course it is impossible to prove a connection between the two events. But when that sort of thing happens, it's no wonder people get rajed up.

Faggo: It all started off with joyriding, people getting chases off the police and ramming them. I never ever done that, like, but I knew that they'd do it just to get back at the police 'cos the police used to raj them up.

I think as you get older you just chill out; you don't want anything to do with it. I wouldn't go out and pinch a car and joyride it and make nothing out of it, would you? But that's what some of these young 'uns were doing. At the time I would have gone out and pinched a car if I was making money off it, which is what a lot of people were doing instead of just joyriding them.

I've been done for TWOC and attempted TWOC [author's note: Yes, I know you're all going to say, 'We know what "TWOC" is', but what about the poor bastards that don't? Oh, OK then, I'll let them work it out for themselves or ask a policeman] but mainly driving while disqualified.

I was banned for 18½ years; they said I tried to run them over! Which was a load of crap. They said I came down a steep hill at 90mph and around a sharp bend at the bottom. I mean, Nigel Mansell couldn't go around that bend at the speed I was supposed to have done. They said I handbraked it and played 'chicken' with them, and then they said they bailed the car and I chased them over the grass. I got banned for six years for that one and got 18 months in jail, but I can say I never done that.

It would be easy for me to say, 'Yeah, I did that, it was fucking great, I made them run, I really showed them,' but I didn't do it, so me saying it now, years later, shows some truth in it. That never happened, they were pure liars and if they wanted you in jail then they'd put you away.

I've got no arguments over a fair cop, but look at the way the police have double standards. I recall years ago a load of coppers from Felling were screwing shops and shifting the gear. They were all done for it in the end but they were liars then. They said that they were guarding the burgled shop when, in fact, they were doing it over themselves. Maybe you could do an article on them being the first police ramraiders. Doesn't that prove the police tell lies? I mean, they can't have one law for themselves and one law for criminals; they lose respect from the paying punters – the taxpayers.

I used to raj the police up on a night-time. I think, if you drive about all night, they raj you up. They just don't want you on the street, do they? Since I've been done for conspiracy, I can own up to having used a scanner; way back then even the police didn't know what a scanner was.

They used to come up over the scanner, 'Faggo's just passed.' I used to think, 'Where's he?' I used to look for him and I'd hear, 'He's pulled in the car park, he's pulled alongside 'es, HE'S ALONGSIDE 'ES.' So we used to brae on the side of the van, 'We know you're there ...' and the copper used to come to the window. 'Have you got the time?' we'd say.

They used to pull me in the car and jack it up and all sorts. So I'd hear them say, 'He's got a back light off.' So I used to pull up in front of them and fix the light. I'd hear, 'He's purposefully gone through a red light.' I used to wonder where they were; they used to be hiding in vans and cars and all that. I was aware of the police surveillance. They knew who was doing ramraids, they knew a few of them, but they had to catch them.

The police seemed incapable of catching ramraiders; they weren't geared up for such a thing, and they were having to do hard work. The police were even working in the street carrying out covert operations. If scruffy-looking geezers, police in disguise, had approached us and said, 'You haven't a couple of leather coats or Berghauses to sell, have you?' then maybe we'd have been caught. They never did this, they were just working in the street and watching us, but we knew they were there, we had scanners and we could hear them.

Even pulling into the petrol station, there'd be four big blokes with bats. You thought you were gonna get chinned, you thought they were gangsters, but they weren't, they were SPG [Special Patrol Group]. They used to drive around in Cosworths and that, no markings on them.

The coppers would be suited or tracksuited up and in T-shirts; you didn't know who the fuck they were. You sussed out who they were when you heard them on the scanner. They'd pull you over saying, 'We've had a report that you've got a shotgun in the boot,' and then they'd rip your car to pieces looking for anything from gloves to scanners and what have you.

I've lost loads of scanners by having them taken off me. You're allowed to carry one but it was a no-no to home in on the police channels. If you were caught with one and it came through with the police channels on them, it was taken off you. We didn't ever find out what happened to them once they'd been taken off us.

The shops that were selling these things, though, didn't give a fuck. Some scanners we bought showed pictures on the boxes of police and ambulances; they were more or less encouraging people to buy these scanners. I had my first scanner in 1985; there were only two other people I knew who had them.

I tried to get the frequency numbers from a certain person but they wouldn't give me them so I had to fiddle with it and get the numbers, just put it on scan and they'd soon lock into frequencies used. Nobody really knew what a scanner was. I had a big home base 1,000-channel scanner; you only really needed a 10-channel scanner at the time, which I also had. It sat on the dash of my car with loads of little buttons on it. The police used to look in my car and they didn't have a clue what it was. I just used to say it was a mobile phone because that's what mobile phones looked like then. Later on, though, they got wise to it; somebody had clued them up on it. That was in about 1989. We just used to sit and listen to it as a novelty; we never really did anything then.

Anonymous: The scanner was a lifesaver, a jailsaver! You had to have a scanner so you knew what was going on. Say you were going along a bypass, you pulled on at a roundabout, and they'd have somebody at the next roundabout blocking it off, waiting for you. You had to have a scanner so you knew when to turn off. But they got wise to that;

they'd have little words for different things so as to confuse you. Now it's all scrambled mish-mash so you can't hear it.

At the time I wouldn't go in a car if I didn't have a scanner. At that time a scanner was about a hundred quid, but you knew you could go out and make that, and more than that. That's if you got the proper graft. It didn't always go according to what you'd set out to do. Sometimes you needed luck to be on your side.

You could also buy a scanner with a mic. If you were sitting in the house, they [other gang members] could be sitting outside and saying, 'This is PC ... we're going to raid ...' They'd be sitting in the car while whoever was in the house would be running all over the shop getting rid of stuff and then looking out the door and seeing their pals in the car. That's what they used to do, and then they used to shite themselves because they thought they were going to get raided. It was just a wind-up really, rajing each other and that.

People thought we were coining it in, but to start with it wasn't fortunes, it wasn't even dole money. You could go out and make five grand or you could go out and make fifty quid.

Sometimes things didn't go to plan; it all depended where you hit really. I've seen teams go out to good graft and come back with nothing. Sometimes it's come on top straight away or it's taken a bit longer to get in. Speed of access would be the main point.

If the place was Currys or Comet or somewhere like that, we'd go and have a look at it and see how easy it was. Most of the time it was just glass panels on the doors. You could get in within seconds, a big sledgehammer, and boosh! Tap the glass in the middle and just kick the rest out around it, and the whole panel used to come out.

With something like a big plate-glass window, maybe you'd just push the bumper up against it and the whole window would fall like a big lump of plastic, 'cos they were plastic in the middle of them or something. Some used to hit it and it could slide down and chop your head off – you had to be careful.

I've seen some people get gashes with them smashing the glass when it's slid and caught them on the arm or something, or even when they're jumping in or out – there's always somebody gets cut. It paid to wear a padded jacket, a nice Berghaus!

The sort of clothes we used to wear depended on the climate. Summer wear for the ramraider would be trainers, tracksuit bottoms, a hooded top often came in handy, a smother and turtles. Winter wouldn't cause us much grief, as it was just a padded jacket over the top of it. All the clothing was dark coloured.

If we were doing a job out of the area we'd pull up in a garage and pay for the juice; we didn't want half the law in the area looking for us before we'd even done the job. If we were doing a job on our own doorstep then it was a simple case of filling up and nashing off, so you didn't pay for it.

A run, Gateshead to Morpeth, wouldn't see us pull into a garage, put a tenner in and blow out 'cos they'd get straight on the radio and say there was a choredy car blew out, and they'd give a description and if it was a high-performance motor the police used to have it blasted all over the area and nationally. If the motor wasn't high performance then it would only be reported locally, and after three days it used to go out nationally. We knew how they worked, so we had to play by their rules.

Some of the stuff I've seen nicked by ramraid gangs would even put Hoults Removals to shame. I've seen people in Luton vans pull up outside three-piece suite warehouses on a Sunday afternoon and just take what they wanted – the shops weren't open on a Sunday then.

I've seen a big cargo wagon being stolen just to be used to transport stuff from big warehouses. The wagon would be driven into the loading bay and loaded up with nine three-pieces. They were all put in a one-bedroom house and the wagon was dumped. People were picking which one they wanted and within a few hours the whole lot was sold. News spread fast and there wasn't any evidence left lying about. People who'd never been able to afford a new three-piece suddenly could. Never mind them offers of buy now and pay later!

There were punters all over ready and willing to buy hoisty swag. People knew who did the ramraids and they used to wait for you to come in so they could get cheap gear. A lot of the people were hard up so in a way we were seen as Robin Hood characters; so long as the stuff was cheap no one gave a fuck where it came from. They used to phone up and say, 'What ye's got?'

We used to go for videos and we used to get about thirty between two or three of us. They used to sell for £80 upwards all day long because they were expensive videos. Then a video would knock you back a few quid, now you'd be lucky to get £30 for one. It sharp mounted up, so two or three of you had a good score.

At times, just driving about you could score on spec. During the day you might go out and look for it. Three of you would pile in the car, pull into the garage, get your scran and cruise about all day. You'd see warehouses with the backs open and people delivering stuff, and you used to think, 'Well, there's something there, we'll try that.' If you got something it was a bonus, if you were lucky that is. You had to try because if you had a good team you knew you were going to make something, and you knew that if it was a good team you weren't going to get caught.

We thought we were invincible; we used to tell the police that we'd be out that night grafting. We knew we were gonna get away with it. Everybody was at it. I've seen kids who haven't got a clue, honest, they'd go and pinch an old Ford Cortina, which even by our standards was old. They'd drive down the Metro Centre and hit Toys R Us or something and pinch about three Scalextric just for the hell of it. I've even seen them go down the to a high-street area, spot a hi-fi and say, 'That's a nice hi-fi,' and go back down and boosh the window out just for the hi-fi. They'd do garages that closed at about 11pm and they'd pinch the tabs out of the tab machine; they wouldn't think about doing the store room.

The middle of Newcastle, Binns department store on a bend in the road, the police station entrance is just yards away from it. That was hit on a Friday night and loads of people were walking by. A Sierra Cosworth hit it and a Carlton GSi 24-valver was ready to fill up as the police were running up the road.

What you've gotta do for the preparation is get some plastic bins because you're gonna need them to carry the stuff – perfumes and other stuff. You just rack the stuff into the bins and run to the car and unload, run in for more and do the same again.

We flew across the river Tyne over the High Level Bridge, drove past the police station and around to Binns store. One car reversed into the door. The back quarter was used on the double glass doors, they were pushed open and the two drivers stayed in the cars. By this time there were people gathered around, shouting, 'Go on, go on!'

What we'd do was throw a few perfumes about and people would pick them up and think, 'This is great.' While they're distracted, the cars are being filled up; one of us would keep the crowd happy by throwing them the odd perfume like bananas to a monkey. This used to happen at a number of other places – we'd have to keep the crowd happy, and we did.

The Cosworth nashed off. The clutch on the Carlton was starting to go and as we went over the High Level Bridge we could see the Cosworth being chased across the Redheugh Bridge by two cruisers, so that was a lucky escape as we couldn't have outrun a cruiser with a slipping clutch.

As our Carlton got by a block of flats, the others in our car said, 'Just drop us off here,' as their arses were starting to go. The driver said, 'I fucking know you are, if I'm getting caught then you'll get caught along with me.' We got the car back from there to the secret hideaway garage at Washington; it was revving its knackers out but it made it doing no more than 30mph.

We scored about a grand apiece off the perfume. We were lucky to get shot of it as it was usually a job to handball out; tabs were the best seller and looking at the price of the things now I'd say they were still a number-one seller. You had to locate the buyer for them before you got the stuff, otherwise it wasn't worth it – our punters couldn't pay half bat for expensive perfumes.

When we did electrical shops over we used to stack

videos up in fours and run out with that pile and back again. With the snout, we used to carry three 5,000 packs or 6,000 packs at a time stacked on top of each other to save running in and out.

There have been times we've been jammed in by the police, but as I've already said you have to push them not ram them. If the radiator's pagerred the car overheats and then you're knackered, you've got to let your car touch theirs, then accelerate and push. You've got to be careful, you're front end could cave in, you could knack your front wheel, and you've got to know that if your the driver 'cos their job is to get everyone away. But not everyone thinks like that, do they? They just start ramming the police car or reversing into them to knacker their radiator. That's what it was all about – to get away.

You did what you did to get away and if the police were up the back end of the car then you'd stop and a few would get out and put the police car window out. The police would reverse back just to stop the chase. If you're going too berserk at 90mph and through red lights and that then they're supposed to abandon the chase because it starts to endanger the public.

Faggo: In my opinion there were only three police drivers at that time that would ram you and they were shit hot. When I got locked up they'd come to my cell and say, 'We knew it was you, we just wanted to catch you.' Some even showed me respect.

Anonymous: These three police drivers would even chase you through red lights at 90mph; they might slow down a little. I've known them to ram people and push them into things, so they did do such things, they can't say they didn't because they did.

The day the helicopter was brought into play it nobbled us. I remember a chase we were involved in. We were in this country lane and down one side was a shear drop. A law car was sitting over the brow of a hill. We seen someone on a radio and soon found out it was the busies, so I reversed back. The police car was trying to ram us over the top. I was flat out and eventually did a reverse turn, into first and away.

We eventually got on the big roundabout on the Washington Highway and there were cruisers sitting there. We were in an Astra 16-valve so I had to go around the roundabout a couple of times to see where I was going to go. I went over a grass verge on to a motorway with no lights on. We turned off a roundabout; one of the lads went, 'Left, left, left.' So I've gone left when I shouldn't have done, I should have kept going the way I was going. Just my fucking luck, there were cruisers and then there was the helicopter from over the town.

I got chased down this country road and then the helicopter just came on top with the lights shining on the road. The low and high beam on the headlights was fucked so I thought, 'Cushty, I can see where I'm going now.' We were losing the police and that, we were doing 80s, 90s and 100mph and that.

The helicopter was with us all the way, the beam was showing the way and then I can remember this farmhouse. I had to brake, I braked hard. Someone again shouted, 'Left, left, left.' I missed the turning, as I didn't know where I was. The front end on the car dropped and collapsed – it was goosed!

So they bailed it. There was a bit of confusion going on as the helicopter light usually stays with the driver, but everyone was diving out of any door that was fucking open. One of the kids who got out shouted, 'If you start it, pick me up ...' That's what he was shouting as he was running. In a situation like that it's each man for himself, there's no shame in doing a runner when it's bang on top. Faggo was the last one out so obviously the helicopter stayed with him thinking he was the driver.

Faggo: The police were miles away, smoke was coming out the sides of the wheels and all sorts. I jumped over a fence and the helicopter was following me. I had a baly and gloves and I buried them in a pile of cow shit. I ran around this building about three times then I jumped in the stable. There was this big shire horse so I was thinking, 'I'll jump on that and fly over there,' this open field and into the woods.

Some of the others were on a curfew imposed by the

courts so I had to go in a different direction to give them a chance to get away. I later found out that they got into a lake and covered themselves so they were OK. They couldn't be found because they weren't giving off any heat being in the lake, so it fucked the helicopter's night camera. I tried to hide myself under the shite when I got around the corner, but the helicopter just stayed on me so I put my hands up and walked to the middle of the field and then walked all the way back and sat on the wall.

The police cars were just driving past me, they couldn't see me, but the helicopter (India 99) eventually directed them in and I was caught. I couldn't get away. I could have had a difficult time if I was identified as the driver, but one of the coppers said, 'I know him, I positively identify you as being one of the passengers in the back of that car.' I said, 'That's right, I was.' All I then faced was a charge of allowing myself to be carried. So they never looked for any gloves or smothers.

I was taken to Felling Police Station. They said, 'Just admit it, admit you were in that car and you'll be out by 11 o'clock.' I said, 'I know I was, I admit it.' So I've done the statement saying I was in the back of the car, 11 o'clock came and I got on the bell and I said, 'Here, what's happening? I'm supposed to be out by eleven.'

They kept me there until the next morning and questioned me about a robbery from Whickham. I thought, 'They're fucking mad, aren't they?'

GRAFTING

This happened about three months before we faced the court on the ramraid charges, so this was carried over for that appearance. I faced a slap on the wrist for this offence and hopefully a walk-out from the court on the other serious charges I faced.

All was going well; the police were hitting brick walls faster than a demolition ball; nothing could touch us, and then this young lass, Ann Haig, came on the scene. I always felt she was one of these users; so long as she was getting whatever for herself then fuck anybody else. She wanted to be part of it all.

I hardly knew her. She was always around one of the gang's home and when they were flashing money her eyes used to light up. For a young girl she was well ahead of her time, but still immature as to what was what.

CHAPTER SEVEN

SHOPPED FOR SHOPPING

BETRAYAL IS USUALLY the first downfall of all whom become involved in crime. Call it by many other names – grassing, informing, stool pigeon, selling out, Judas, traitor – it all boils down to the same thing. Being shopped by an outsider, a good citizen, to some extent can be comprehended, but being shopped by an insider makes for a complicated set of thoughts.

The gang couldn't be stopped; the police were ineffective and were hitting a brick wall. Although they knew the gang responsible for the biggest hauls and the most damage caused, proving it was going to be difficult. It was a stroke of luck that brought the balance of power to the side of the see-saw that the police were on.

It all pivoted on one person's testimony and information – 16-year-old Ann Haig. It was claimed that her reason for turning informant was that catalogue payments had been missed for an agency she ran. One of the ramraiders was supposedly messing her about with payments for a fireplace.

Continuing on from the last chapter, we have Faggo and another member of a ramraid gang who wishes to remain anonymous. Here we go:

Faggo: Ann Haig was going out with two members of a ramraid gang at the same time, because when we were eventually at court and in the dock it came out that she was going out with a couple of them and all the lasses were sitting saying, 'It better not be my gadgy, I'll fucking kill him if it is.' I was saying, it's not me, but she did get accused of going with one of them, and one of them *was* going with her. Ann Haig had a common bond by calling in to see one of the gang's lasses. (Joanne Bewick was mentioned in a feature in *Take a Break* magazine and was the name given by Ann Haig as being the girlfriend of one of the ramraid gang's organisers, Brian Richardson.)

I mean, there was this Ann lass, she was flying around on roller skates with hot pants up her arse while she was eight months' pregnant. You can't tell me that was normal or even decent. She had her own flat at 16 years of age and was living on her own, as she'd fallen out with her boyfriend. Her friend since being a kid was Joanne. I'm not saying anything that hasn't been said or written about already as the magazine piece spilled the beans on this, and this, as far as I know, was against her best friend who she even accused of trying to sell her stolen goods supposed to be from the ramraids.

When you see the magazine article you'll see for yourself the lies she spun to get £250 for the interview. She made out that butter wouldn't melt in her mouth. She was running a catalogue, a mail-order agency, so it seems she'd bent the rules to get such an agency, as apparently you have to be at least 18 years old to get one.

So there she is with her questionable agency trying to flog stuff to Joanne. She then goes on to say that Joanne ordered £500 worth of stuff and in return Joanne rushed around home and came back with blankets, toys and ornaments to sell her in return. All of this was in the magazine article, openly admitted by Ann Haig. She was as bent as a five-bob note and when she appeared in court she was made out to be some little saint.

The best part was that Ann said she wasn't interested in dodgy stuff – what a fucking divvy! You can't tell me you're less than squeaky clean running a questionable catalogue agency, and then when cheap goods are offered you suddenly get an attack of 'I want a good citizen's award' – pull the other one.

Ann freely admitted that she couldn't stand Joanne's 'loud-mouthed' boyfriend, Brian – who she classed as one of the gang leaders. She went on to say in this article that Brian had to have Joanne help him to read the Yellow Pages looking for places to turn over, as he could barely read. Come on, Brian is supposed to be running a gang and clever enough not to get caught and yet he's not supposed to be able to read?

My theory is Ann saw money lying around and she just wanted some for herself. She was a small-time criminal herself and a self-confessed fraudster. She freely admitted telling lies to social services in order to get money she wasn't entitled to, she admits that in the article. I mean, I'm not a grass and if it wasn't there in black and white I wouldn't be saying this, but it is, so I am.

She made out that catalogue money owed to her was being missed by Joanne, even though, she says, she'd seen a couple of grand sitting on the shelf in Joanne's flat. She made on that she'd had to call time and time again and was supposedly told by Joanne that she was skint even though this couple of grand was sat there on the shelf. She should tell stories for a children's magazine.

She says that this pissed her off so she shopped Bri to the busies, saying that all the stuff from a raid on Provident's warehouse was lying about his house. Funny though, the police never found anything to connect the raid on the Provident warehouse when they raided the following day.

Even after this story about the catalogue money,

Ann said she patched things up with Joanne over the non-payment. Why, then, was Ann remembering every detail, as she says, when it supposedly wasn't until the police called on her for her own little enterprise she had going? Why was Ann Haig part of the furniture in Joanne's living room long before she shopped the gang? She'd been part of the neighbourhood and was even a statistic as a single teenage parent. In my opinion she did it because she was cornered and, for someone of only 16 years of age being confronted by two CID officers for questioning, it gave her no choice. She got out of it the only way she knew how; she betrayed her lifelong friend, Joanne Bewick. Who needs enemies with someone like her as a friend?

I spotted her in a car with the law. She gave an excuse, saying it was connected to her dole fiddle, last of the big rip-off merchants – it was for £25, that's all. You've got a whole police force trying to catch ramraiders around the north-east and here's this 16-year-old has to do it for them. If that was me running the police, I'd be embarrassed by it all. The top and bottom of it all is that some of the lads were a little bit used to talking in front of her. Me, I didn't trust her as far as I could spit, that's how it was. Unless you were a face then, as far as I was concerned you could fuck off.

I told the rest of the gang that she'd grassed on us and after the law were seen going into her flat it was a bit more of a coincidence, so everyone stopped the planning of raids. It was going to be her word against everyone else's, one person's word against half a dozen or maybe more if it came on top and we were to be lifted. We knew she'd been taken away by the law for her own safety and all we could do was sit tight.

Judging by the magazine article, the police got plenty of overtime out of it while staying in a cosy hotel with her and interviewing her from 7am to 10pm, or so the article led us to believe. Come off it! I can't see anyone sitting there for 15 hours a day for a couple of weeks passing information to the police, but that's what the article said, so it must be true!

Another load of cobblers was when she'd said that Bri had tried to mow her down in a car. There she was walking along, carrying her baby, and Bri's supposed to drive straight at her. Suddenly she turns into Cat fucking Woman and jumps a wall to safety; pull the other one, it's got bells on. I've never read such a parcel of shite in my whole life, man.

You should have read some of the other newspaper reports when we were all lifted. They had a field day and as usual they have to make someone the hero of the day, and that particular day it was Ann Haig's turn. In court, Ann was accused by defence barristers of shopping us all out of spite, because she wasn't given anything out of the Provident warehouse raid, which was more like it. She was even accused in court of storing some of the hoisty gear in her house and of having a sexual relationship with a gang member – she denied all of this.

She was all dressed up and innocent looking; she should have been in the dock with us. Bri's lass, Joanne, got two years' probation for letting her home be used as a base. I mean, fancy shopping your best mate just like that. I believe she'd been paid for the catalogue stuff but she was greedy and wanted some of the money and other things attached to our gang; she wanted to be known amongst her friends as a face.

She gave her information and then that was it, she was on her own. Do you know, she even had to get money, I think it was £500, from Cowies of Sunderland (Cowies Motor Group) to help carpet her hideaway safe house out.

Do you know, she even wrote to Captain Cash in one of the national newspapers – what a fucking cheek! There were no flies on her. I said what she was like, anything for money.

> Dear Cap'n,
> I'm 17 and in hiding after helping to nail
> a gang of ramraiders. I couldn't go back
> home and my furniture, my clothes and
> year-old baby's things were stolen.
> (The letter secured a helping hand from
> Cap'n Cash and a cheque was sent.)

Author's note: As a consequence of Ann Haig informing on the ramraid gangs, ten men and two women were committed by Gateshead magistrates for trial at the Crown Court on charges of conspiracy to commit ramraids: Brian Richardson, Richard 'Faggo' Dodd, Michael Quinn, Warren Patterson, Alan Hutton, Brendan Spillane, Philip McDonald, Alan Williams, Anthony Wheatley, David Richardson, Diane Richardson and Joanne Bewick.

(As time went on more names would be added to the charge sheets and many other spin-off inquiries would take place as a direct consequence of Ann Haig's involvement with the gang.)

Anonymous: Everybody knew about the ramraids, but since people were scoring they didn't want it to end. Brian Richardson had just got a new flat and he was blowing all his money on doing it up the way he wanted it: nice big leather three-piece, big fires and all that. If you were doing something then you had to have the very best of everything, the best tracksuit, the best trainers, the best luxuries, plenty of tom, big chains and necklaces, bracelets and big fucking rings. You can't survive on a giro, can you?

Ann Haig was always hanging around Brian Richardson's and she was going with one of Brian's pals. She was there more than she was at her own place. She heard one of them saying that they were gonna do Post Offices so, because of that, there were three Post Office charges laid at the gang's door. I mean, I think this lass Haig dressed like an unmade bed so I suppose I can go with her reason for being pissed off when, at times, she didn't get anything from the raids.

They were pulling five hundred quids out here and there so she was making on she hadn't had her catalogue money, even though I believe she had. But what she'd done was spent it and bumped the catalogue, and said she wasn't getting paid off them for the stuff, which I think was a load of shite really. I reckon she was spending the money. My theory is the catalogue must have written to her saying, where's the money? She'd blown it and she was going and seeing her bairn's father.

This was Haig's chance to grab her 15 minutes of fame. Maybe she wanted the attention that the gang had received and she felt left out. Maybe some shrink can work it all out. She'd suddenly changed into this superbitch and the power went to her head. With all the attention she was getting it didn't help us, she was too familiar with a lot of things she didn't know about and that proved to me that we were being taken for mugs by the law, but we knew what was going on.

There was a van there and one got caught – it was John Hall. He's since been murdered, got shot in the head as he was walking down a back lane.

John asked for some graft. 'Any graft or what?' We

used to have people begging us to go. Hall got his collar felt first time; the kids left him and drove off. He ended up with a 12-month sentence; he was there with his mother's marigold gloves on and his mother's stockings over his head.

He was skint and he said, 'I'll come with you'se.' But the coppers were waiting; they'd had their card marked. All these people that used to graft together had known each other for years, everybody knew everybody else. You knew who was all right and who wasn't! You knew who you could trust then, but now you don't.

If you were a grass, nobody would bother with you then. They'd say, 'Fuck that,' or you'd get your car smashed up or whatever, but now if you're a grass they'll pat you on the back and take you for a fucking pint. We used to have somebody at the airport phoning us up saying, 'The helicopter's in,' and once it was in, it had to be in for eight hours. So then you knew you had eight hours to graft in.

Our ramraid times used to differ. Sometimes we'd be out at four o'clock in the morning, six o'clock in the morning or as soon as it got dark at 5.30.

I've seen someone pull on the High Street and do a chemist over and that's as soon as it's shut, loading up with perfume. There's people standing at bus stops and everything, but they just stood. But now there are too many heroes, that's what'll knack you now. Too many people chucking tins of pears and beans at you and the like.

Ramraiding was brilliant, but when I used to go I always used to take some bog roll with me. Everyone wanted a shite before graft, so everyone used to take their bog roll with them. The hardest part was getting the car out of the garage without being spotted; the garages were in some raj places. It's what they call the 'fight or shite' (flight) syndrome.

You couldn't find a garage what was a hundred per cent, so you used to go to the garage and get the car out. Everybody hated going to the garage, that was the hardest bit, 'cos you didn't know where they were going to be. They'd sit in the garage, wait for you to go in and then they'd pounce on you where it was pitch black so you couldn't see.

So once you pull the car out – butterflies. I used to get butterflies, me. Once I'd done the damage it was like an everyday thing, it was just a job really; I was as calm as anything. Even getting the chase from police didn't bother me. We used to carry our own music cassettes, put the tape in and listen to our favourite tunes – rave music or something and let it blast – and go to graft and sit outside the shop with the music blasting, fucking mental!

If the police were behind you I used to flip the mirror. I didn't want to know what was behind; I wanted to know what was happening up front. You'd just forget about them when they got behind you and lose them because they were shite, but then they started getting Cosworths just for up here. There was one sure way to fuck them up; by using something like a hot-hatch turbo you could lose the big Cosies around back lanes no bother. So they still couldn't catch the ramraiders, then they got a high-powered Escort – still no fucking good.

I remember when we were up for our committals, we took the old-style committal where it was up to the prosecution to prove the case. As well as that, it would force their hand to show us what they had up their sleeve, if anything at all. That's when all the charges were being brought up against us and all the evidence and the witnesses.

That Ann Haig comes in, from the tramp what she was they'd smartened her up as though she was a young lady and all that, calling the police by their first names and on friendly terms with them.

Our solicitor was getting on her case, bringing her down to what she was. She had already accused two solicitors of being involved with the purchase of ramraiding goods, one of whom she couldn't even identify – that's how clever she was. So if she got this part wrong, how could the rest of her evidence be relied on? She was an arrogant thing; she even stood outside of the court room looking arrogant. They even had coppers on the roof of the magistrates' court to make it look good – it was like a circus.

Faggo: It was about 6.30am and the door was kicked in. Young Richard was only seven weeks old and they found one Berghaus coathanger in the cupboard. I told my barrister that it was planted, but it made no difference.

They found a bath-mat set that they claimed was from the Provident warehouse raid. It had no stickers on, nor did it have any other identifying marks. They took my Sky and satellite and all that. They said they were from the Team Valley Trading Estate job. It was Joanne Bewick, Bri Richardson's lass, who said it was from there. She even said Bri was the ringleader and anything he said was done – she got him seven years behind bars.

He got an extra 12 months more than anyone else, but there were no gaffers on the job. If there were any gaffers it would have been me and Bri, sort of thing. Me and Bri used to go out looking around together. We weren't gaffers, we were just grafters really. The law found ten jemmy bars in the cupboard; this kid gave me them. They were brand spanking new. He said, 'There's some jemmies for you.' I thought they might come in handy. The law practically cleared our home out, oil paintings, a leather Chesterfield three-piece suite ... They pulled an ornate fireplace off the wall and damaged it, damaged the three-piece and left my family with nothing.

I was remanded in local custody for a week; the

whole lot of us were spread across the region in different police stations. I was charged with one ramraid as a holding charge and then over the week they gathered loads of evidence and, next thing I knew, I was charged with three Post Office robberies across the region.

You know when you lift your eyes to say 'Fuck off, man'? The copper woman said, 'You've just lifted your eyebrows up, what have you done that for?' You know, to get me to talk. I just sat and said nothing. Even when they said, 'Identify yourself for the tape,' it was my solicitor who had to do it for me. He had to say, 'Mr Dodd is in the room,' and stuff like that because I didn't say one fucking word, because I didn't know what anybody else was saying, as well as the fact that I wasn't going to be saying anything anyway.

The others that were arrested and locked up were tripping themselves up by saying things, not intentionally, and that's why I never said anything. It would be so easy to say something that could be taken the wrong way.

There were all sorts of rumours flying around that different companies had given Ann Haig £30,000 in total as reward for her part in the trial, but how true that is I don't know. Other things had gone on involving companies declaring bigger losses than actually took place.

There were big companies on the Team Valley that

got hit and it was claimed they were saying there was a large amount of tabs taken – really! They could have kidded me, but I don't want to go into it. But I'll stand by what I say, our gang in that particular raid took no tabs. Anywhere that was hit was claiming a whole boat load more than what was taken. You tell me who the real crooks are?

There were some very big companies involved and all had very large insurance claims in. Doesn't that tell you something?

Ramraid gangs were doing these places a favour and they made people plenty of money from the dodgy insurance claims that were put in. Ann Haig was all part of the same thing; she didn't just pluck names out of thin air, how could she remember all the names, places and dates of supposed ramraids? She wasn't that clever; devious yes, clever no! From day one she was getting visits from the police and she was very familiar with some of them.

I had that many charges I didn't know if I was coming or going. I was even charged with an attempted murder on a guy called Dougie Moore, but that was dropped with a load of other bollocks. I was supposed to have bitten Dougie Moore's ear off and he nearly died as a consequence of the loss of blood. That case got chucked.

From what I hear, it was a case that Moore had nicked some ramraiders' Cosie full of leather coats and one of them collared him some while later and bit his ear off. He was just a joyrider and had opportunely taken their car. They caught up with him and he suffered the consequences. What made it worse for him was that I'd learned that he hadn't gone to hospital, and had lost a lot of blood.

The next thing I know, I was told by a busy that I had to hand myself in at a cop shop in Felling. So I went there and little Bri Richy and Quincy were also there. We were told that we'd be out by nine o'clock that night. We were charged with something or other and bailed out, so we knew they were watching us for the ramraids, plus I had a fine, and if you get locked up when you've got a fine you're kept for the courts the next day. So when I was bailed out, I knew it was on top and all the planning for ramraids was stopped.

Moore was banged up in the same prison as us and he made it known he didn't want the charge pursued so it was all dropped. It got discontinued at the magistrates' court and that was the end of it. Why my name was thrown in I don't know. So there I was, just cleared of an attempted murder wrap, one charge down and God knows how many robbery charges in front of me.

We were told to expect between 9 and 14 years. By that time we'd been on remand from 6 January, but I was JRd [Judge's Remand], which was for the reckless driving. I was found guilty and was giving an 18-month prison sentence and a six-year driving ban – so I was found guilty and waiting for reports of sentencing. It worked in my favour 'cos I was sentenced for that with the ramraid sentence.

We were back and forward from prison to court every week until we had our old-style committal and then we were there every day. And then we had to also be taken to another court to have the Dougie Moore rap dropped. We might as well have spent our time living in the courts' cells for the length of time we were in them.

It does your head in and I'm sure that's what it's designed for. That sort of thing shouldn't go on. I mean, you should've seen the time we were having to get up in the prison – I just don't do mornings.

There doesn't seem to have been much evidence, other than Ann Haig's say-so. At the old-style committal I had the Post Office robberies, another five robberies for something else and four burglaries on commercial premises chucked.

We all thought, 'This is it, we're going to walk here.' Haig's evidence counted for nothing; we were going to be free. We were all done for conspiracy, fucking conspiracy! The police should have got it right in the first place. Shows you how poor their case was, and on the basis of that we should have all walked, but no, they had to have another bite at the cherry!

Once tried and charges are dismissed, that should be it, but no!

Ann Haig was a compulsive liar; a shoplifter and she'd been proven to be a liar, yet she was allowed to give her evidence. Quincy [Michael Quinn] had to put his hands up; his statement wasn't too good and would have gone against the rest of us so he had to take the fall. Everybody was calling each other grasses when in jail. Each day one was offered a deal to plead 'guilty' to this and that, and if so then they'd only get a small sentence, if you'd call four years a small sentence!

Warren Patterson was doing two years anyway so he took the four stretch, Alan Hutton got five years, Brendan Spillane got five years, Quincy and me got six years apiece – the 'two lieutenants' that's what they called us – and Bri Richardson got seven years. A total of 33 years.

They were telling us we could get 18 years each if we pleaded 'not guilty'. That's what our own barristers were telling us; they had us flapping and, looking back over it, I believe that's what they had wanted to have happen to us, fucking tossers.

There were three of us left in the dock: there was me, Alan Williams and Phil McDonald. I was going 'not guilty' all the way, that was my plan. The deal put to me was that if I entered a plea of 'guilty' then the other two would be kicked out. So I said I wanted a visit from my wife. I said to Mandy, 'What will I do?

They've offered me six years and if I take it the other two walk.' I thought to myself, 'I've done 12 months' [JR] so it would leave three years to serve if I behaved myself, and not counting parole I'd soon be out.'

My concern at that point was that I could end up with 14 years if I was found guilty. So I took the six. I thought I'd serve my time with the remainder of my co-accused, but I ended up being shipped out from Durham to Yorkshire. I would have to get my head down and serve the time as best I could. In terms of prison sentences imposed, mine wasn't the biggest in the world, but when you want to be free then even a single day can seem like a lifetime.

Of course, I asked my brief to ask what the chances of an appeal would be on the severity of sentence. I knew my chance of winning an appeal on my 'guilty' plea was an insane idea, so I waited in hope. My sentence might as well have been one of a life sentence – it felt that way.

Word came back that counsel's advice was not to appeal against severity of sentence and that the six years imposed on me was at the lower end of the scale to be expected for such offences.

I was given a concurrent sentence for my driving charges. David Callan, my counsel, said in the advice on appeal, 'I would be loath to encourage Mr Dodd in what I would consider would be a wholly hopeless appeal, for fear that this may adversely affect his remission.' There it fucking was in black and white, staring me in the face; my only hope now was that I'd get some jam role [parole].

When it all sunk in I was quite a way through my time and my thoughts were of my family, waiting outside.

Anonymous: When we were on remand I used to tell people to go out and do ramraids and tell them how easy it was. I'd promote the idea so they'd carry on doing them and it would take the heat off us, and maybe they'd even start wondering if we really had any involvement after all. If we were in jail then they'd think, 'Well, it can't be them, they're in jail.'

People think that a ramraid is where you get a car and ram something – it's not really. A ramraid is more a smash and grab really, you just put the window out. Fair enough, most of the raids involved using cars and trucks; I was running around in 1984 doing ramraids, long before others started doing it. I'd be running around in three-year-old 7 series BMWs, driving for other gangs, working with people older than me, but they wanted me to do mad robberies. But at that time I'd only been to jail for driving while banned so a robbery sentence looked big. Fuck me, though, I should have done one, maybe it would have put me on my feet.

Now, though, there's too many drugs about; there's too much smack. They'd rather go and pinch from an old woman coming home from the bingo so they'd be able to buy a tenner bag of drugs. Cameras and the helicopter didn't worry us so they can't blame them; it's bottle, and they've got no bottle left in them. Now they'd rather go for the easy touch.

I knew a woman who was from Italy. She drove for a London firm, this was going back years and years. She'd just drive the car and that was a woman. Compare that to now. Look at the type of crimes being done, old grannies raped in their own homes by nonces.

At that time the raids gave us a buzz and I'd love winding the busies up. We all thought we were invincible and that nobody could touch us. The busies never caught anyone doing anything. It didn't just happen that we were nicked while doing ramraids. We weren't. It all boiled down to police informers; not a single copper can take credit for us being nicked – no special police skills or covert operations got us nicked.

I know a lot of the lads who got nicked couldn't even pinch a dust cap off a car now, not because they've lost the bottle, but because they've been there, worn the T-shirt and all that. We set the trend – people from all over the area, the country and the world copied these ramraids.

Who can say they were there when it all happened and are still around now from the trends they started? I mean, you can't say safe-cracking started in a certain area, you can't say robberies started in a certain area, but RAMRAIDING fucking started here, in Newcastle – HOWWAY THE LADS!

CHAPTER EIGHT

DOING BIRD

IN THE LAST couple of chapters we covered quite a bit of ground on the outside of prison walls. Now, with the help of Faggo, we explore the goings on from the wrong side of the prison wall, but before we do that I'd like to cover a little bit of the ramraid scene from Liverpool. Readers of Viv and the *Geordie Mafia Vol. 2* will appreciate my fondness for Liverpool, particularly after I covered the club-doorman scene there.

Maybe I could cover a little more if I can get the right story from Curtis Warren; although a book has been written about Curtis so it is a little worrying in what to make of it all.

Maybe, in my opinion, there's one driver in the whole of the UK who could match up to Faggo's prowess behind the wheel, and that's a guy from Liverpool. Stephen Lunt started grabbing the headlines as a 14-year-old when a Crown Court sent him away for four years to a detention centre.

Lunt was in big demand and his driving skills were legendary, certainly a near match for Faggo, but I give Faggo the edge over him as what he could do with two wheels should have made him into a circus act. Talk about the wall of death, that was kiddie's stuff compared to what others have said he could do while on two-wheeled machines. Faggo, though, plays this down.

The Liverpool scene was buzzing with plenty of crime gangs. One particular gang excelled more than others did at the ramraid game. Some Liverpool firms might wish to take credit for the ramraid phenomenon but they were a little behind their cousins in Newcastle, although they still had a pretty respectable outfit going by the sounds of it.

A guy named Paul Uchegbu was running a brand-new BMW, paid for in cash from the proceeds of his involvement with ramraiding. The ramraid gangs in Liverpool would pick cars with sunroofs for their raids. Not so they could take the salute like a four-star general but so they could pelt pursuing police cars with all sorts of heavy objects. Police cars would resemble stock racers after a heavy session of chasing the raiders. If a golf ball wasn't going to put police off then a gun would. It was common for guns to be brandished at the police; nothing like a .38 to put the police off a hot pursuit.

The police in Liverpool had to devise a different method of pursuing the ramraiders and that was going to be from a safe distance high in the sky. In came the police helicopter with all of the standard accessories needed to follow stolen cars in the dead of night. Whatever the police could come up with, it wasn't going to be easy to put the raiders off their stride.

Liverpool Airport was the base for the police helicopter and back then in the late 1980s security wasn't the most important thing in the world. A gang of ramraiders was going to put paid to the helicopter once and for all. The gang arrived on site when all was quite and dark.

Out came the axes and they set about the windows of the 'copter. Considering that the windows were toughened glass, they didn't get very far. Not to be put off by this little setback, they proceeded to throw Molotov cocktails at the thing – still fuck-all happened! It still had seven of its nine lives left as the diesel-filled Molotovs smouldered out, and by this time the crew had been alerted by the ruckus and were starting to investigate the noise.

Ramraiders are very proficient at ramraiding, but such a task of sabotage was best left to the likes of the SAS. If they'd tried the door of the 'copter they would have found it to be unlocked! This shows the different type of thinking required for such a different job to what they were used to. The 'copter was soon back in action and the gang's chances of destroying it were lost. This gang had lots of bottle but very little by way of planning.

When Uchegbu was banged up in Admiral Police Station, it was attacked with a Molotov cocktail – this time, though, full of petrol. It prompted the police to put on a show of strength by having armed officers put in place around the court building. Uchegbu was remanded into custody for vehicle offences and drug possession.

Our friend Stephen Lunt was involved in all of this and, in a similar way that the Newcastle gang were selling stolen clothing and coats, so it was that Lunt would be capture while trying to sell his wares to an undercover cop. Lunt was yanked off the street for his part in this. He got off pretty lightly in being given a one-year custodial sentence. When you consider it was rumoured that Lunt had taken a chase involving police cars and the helicopter from Manchester to Liverpool along the M62, in which a policeman nearly lost his foot after ploughing into the tail of Lunt's car, it would seem he got off very lightly indeed.

The case against Liverpool's ramraid gang was proven and Delroy Showers, the fence, received a five-year sentence, Sonny Boy Osu and Uchegbu received 14 years between them and, of course, Lunt received his one-year contract to serve the Queen in her hotel. A total of 20 years wasn't a bad result, especially since

Sonny Boy Osu was on a bender (suspended sentence) for trying to nick a very expensive sports car worth something in the region of £130,000, a very tantalising piece of equipment by the sound of it.

When we compare how Faggo did his bird to how Sonny Boy Osu and Uchegbu served their time, it makes you wonder why they even bothered jailing Faggo, as it would seem he had a much more interesting lifestyle behind bars than the two aforementioned.

Osu and Uchegbu had the job of steering young offenders away from the evils that lay ahead of them; a programme based on similar successful schemes run in USA prisons was also used in Risley Prison on visiting groups of potential young hoodlums.

Moving on to Faggo's life behind bars, I'll let you drift off into his narration of what it was like for him.

Faggo: The first thing you think of when serving a long prison sentence is about having a visit from your family or your woman. Now that I was weighed off I could see I only had three years ahead of me and Mandy was visiting me so the nine to 14 years I was expecting made me feel good that I only had three to do.

After a while of sitting in the pad it gets boring, nothing to do, so I had it arranged for me to be transferred to Everthorpe Prison in Brough, North Humberside, Yorkshire. I thought, if I can do a couple of years there then it would break my time up.

As it happens I bumped into Bri Richardson down there, but he got shipped out, he was only there a couple of weeks. I fell out with him straight away as soon as I got there over one steroid tablet; that's what it's like in such a place. I had a hundred steroids, he'd used his up, but what I'd done was to hand my steroids out on a visit at Durham because I was moving jails and I would have them handed back in again once settled in my new nick.

When I was in Durham I had a screw wired up to fetch stuff in. Everybody else seemed to be on these steroids and getting bigger so I didn't want to be touching drugs or anything as I never touched drugs before I went to jail – not even cannabis. When I went into jail everybody was having the tack and that. That's when I started with the tack but I thought, 'No! I'll keep a clear head.' Everybody wanted to be big so I got steroids; my first batch was a hundred 50mg Napalon tablets.

I bumped into Bri on the same day I landed at Everthorpe and he immediately asked me for one of my steroid tablets, as he'd run out of his, which he said he'd give me back as soon as he got a visit. I didn't have any so I couldn't give him one. He just fell out with me, but I just put that down to the way the steroids had got to him.

Bri didn't talk to me for about four weeks. When he was in the block though, I still sent him baccy, shampoo and soap regardless of him falling out with me. His so-called pals in the jail turned their back on him and didn't give a fuck. The time came for Bri to be shipped out of Everthorpe and he got a letter to me he'd written in the block, and after that everything was all right.

By this time my steroids had come in and I was starting to put a fair bit of size on. The gym was the place to be, but I soon found another place to be and that was on cloud nine – I started to smoke the happy baccy and soon came off the steroids; too much like hard work, fuck that for a lark, so what if those other fuckers wanted to push metal about all night.

Smoking tack was the in thing. If you weren't smoking tack you were a prune, really, weren't you? You were really like an outcast because that's what everybody did. I then thought that to survive in jail you've gotta deal it, so it wasn't long before I became a baron. I had nothing outside of jail, all that I had was done in by this time so I had to look after myself in there.

My reason for going on the steroids was to be able to put weight on. When I got to Everthorpe there was only a handful of Geordies down there. I'd met a guy who was from Middlesbrough, Mark, and we stuck together, him, this other kid and me. Mark was a big lad. I was padded up with him from Durham and I went to Everthorpe with this kid. I mean, back in the north-east we class Middlesbrough as being in Yorkshire – well, it might as well be – but the minute we were in a different manor we joined up. We were padded up together for a couple of years so if he had a fight I also had a fight sort of thing.

I remember on the wing at Everthorpe, silly fuckers weren't giving a fuck about things; they were setting fire to bins. Well, at six o'clock if you wanted to get a bar in the gym then you had to be at the doors ready to be let out, otherwise the other wings would be there and you'd be left with the shit bars. So the minute the doors opened you had to run like fuck to the gym and grab a bar.

Talk about Germans grabbing all the poolside loungers in Spain, that was nothing compared to this. There'd be cons holding three bars: 'This one's for …' so you'd still be running around in the gym looking for a spare bar. That's all some people lived for in there so, when these rajy jacks were setting fire to the bins in our wing at six o'clock, it meant our wing couldn't be opened up until later, so we weren't getting into the gym until well after every other wing was let out.

We'd be standing about waiting for bars until seven o'clock. The idiots that had set the bins alight were from Halifax, Bradford and places like that. I've got nothing against these lads, but these firelighters were giving them a bad name. Wings were named after saints – Andrew Wing, George Wing and so on. Fuck knows who the patron saint of fire was though.

Anyway, this prison officer was a Geordie. He'd been there for a while. He got Mark and me in his office because we were starting to kick off about the hold-ups. He said, 'Look, if you quieten the wing down you'll have everything your own way, just keep it quiet.' So we ended up bashing the rajies up and all the other cons were turning against them and coming around to our way of thinking.

We'd just go into the pads of these rajies and give them it. You get these long bars of soap in prison, the ones the cleaners use, like the old soap blocks used years ago – one of them in a stocking works wonders. It does the damage does a bar of soap about a foot long.

We might have to use the odd bed leg if we couldn't find a soap bar; these bed legs weren't like the ones you get on a bed in your home, they were a good 18 inches long and were just the right weight to handle. A few whacks with that and they'd soon get the idea. So what if we cracked a few idiots? The place soon picked up and we were always the first lot in the gym after that.

After about six months of being at Everthorpe, people who had come in with me were starting to get home leaves. That's how these prisons work; the only way they can get you to behave is by dangling a good-behaviour carrot. Mark was doing a seven stretch and even he was on a home leave. Muggins here, though, wasn't getting one, and I was having none of it!

If you're inside and you've got family then it's important to keep contact with them otherwise when you get out you could well end up a stranger and you start doing crime again, that's how it's supposed to work. I wanted to be out on a leave; I wasn't any different to the next man but I was being mugged off.

The governor said, 'You can't have a home leave until your first parole date, which is another eight months away.' This governor lived in a motor home outside of the prison. His home was miles away and he was located in this dirty big motor home till he could suss a place out to move his family into. I said to him, 'I know you've got a motor home, that can sharp go walkies, don't fuck me about here, what the fuck have I gotta do to prove myself, man?'

With us doing big sentences, because most of the other cons at Everthorpe were doing 12 months and the like, we were known as the 'Suit Men', that's what they used to call us, 'Suit Men from Newcastle'. I just took it that we were gangsterfied or something like that; I just went along with it. Pull a couple of metal bed legs out and people start to give you a bit of respect.

How I managed to get to Everthorpe was because a screw in Durham Prison pulled me to one side and he says, 'Faggo, there's this kid come in on D-wing, on the ones. I want him bashed because he's tampered with my daughter.' The guy was in on a different charge, killing a dog or something, and he had tampered with this screw's daughter so he was given it good style. Another screw come after that and took us up the hospital to take the kid's kit up because I was the Number One on D-wing, which means I was head orderly and my pad was open most of the time, even on a night time when other cons were locked up.

Being Number One doesn't mean you lick up to the screws, it's a hard job to get. The screws only used to give the job to someone they knew was a hundred per cent and was solid. By solid I mean reliable and knowing all the tricks of the game and not dropping anyone in it. The name of the screw that asked me to sort this nonce out would never be given to anyone by me, and that's what it's all about.

I used to have the run of D-wing and my pad door was open all of the time. It was up to me when I wanted to bang my door up. I had the respect from the screws and cons alike. The guy I'd just put into hospital was now having his gear dropped off by me. That favour I did got me allocated to Everthorpe.

Back to the Everthorpe situation, in which I wanted a home leave that I was entitled to.

I called home and said to Mandy, 'Do you want me home for a night? Pick me up Tuesday morning.' Mandy couldn't believe it and neither could I. That night was the shortest in my life and no sooner was

Mandy picking me up it seemed five minutes had passed and here she was dropping me off again.

After I went back and proved myself to be trustworthy, I was given a category 'C' status, which meant I could be passed for work outside of prison. There I was looking at the biggest set of tits I'd ever laid my eyes on, but they were hanging from a cow and I was responsible for milking 120 cows every day of the week.

One day, after spending six weeks on the cow-milking job, I was called into the office and told that I had been upgraded to a category 'D' status and I had been allocated to Rudgate Open Prison in Wetherby, Yorkshire. My old pal, Mark, from Middlesbrough had already been sent there some weeks earlier so I'd be joining him for some more fun and games.

What happened was, I was told to make my own way from Everthorpe to Rudgate Prison. 'What, you mean I can leave prison and go on my own?' I replied with my eyes wide open. Looking back on it, I thought it was bizarre. Anyway, my mother, father and Mandy picked me up and took me to Rudgate. We had to be there at a certain time, so we just hung around Boston Spa until late morning and I just walked into the jail with my kit, me a ramraider serving six years freely walking into a prison – was I mad?

As soon as I was in the place among the cons' there was two bottles of Pils lager waiting for me and from then on we had drink all of the time. We'd go and pick up the booze drops left nearby, as the fence was only wire mesh and about six feet tall. You'd see the fence had been sewn back together from earlier exit and entry holes; we just used to climb over.

We'd cut the sleeves off our jumpers, tie a knot in it and poke holes in for our eyes, pull it over our heads as a baly and we used to go over the fence and meet this lad for big bags of scran and booze. When we got the stuff back we'd have a party. We used to bring cameras in, take photos and then hand the film out on our next pick-up to be developed.

We used to go over for other people's drops and it would mean we got half the load: baccy, tabs, beer and other stuff. We had this kid who used to do the kiting [chequebook fraud]; he's dead now. We used to phone him up and ask him to meet us; we would pay him with money from the tack we sold so it was worth his while coming down. He was also bringing us tack, which we gave him the money for. The more we sold, the more money we had to buy bigger drops.

Mark and I would get on the roofs of Rudgate, which were little billets, and we'd run along the roof, over to the kitchens and over the football fields and over the fence. Of course, you never knew if some screw would be hiding somewhere so the home-made masks were the business. If we ever did get spotted then it was a quick detour back to the dorm and no screw was gonna risk waking a few hundred tired cons up to find which pair it was. We met the kid in the nearby woods.

Rudgate has a lot of jealousy, people putting notes in the box. I've been there with solicitors, barristers, accountants, magistrates and a whole bunch of ugly-looking critters who could've been in for anything. You can't trust anyone because it's full of fucking nonces; they get told to say they're in for burglary and that, these posh cunts. You were best to stick to your own type.

My job at Rudgate was in the laundry; it was a good job and helped pass the time. I spent my time doing all sorts of things. I was even on the prison football team and when it came to the away matches we actually used to travel to the away team's pitch. So I was getting myself out and about. It was just like the old days in 1984 and 1985 when I was at Rudgate for driving offences and I was on the football team back then as well.

Prisons are unpredictable places. It's always a calm before a storm in those places. You don't relax for a minute, not unless you're in a position to be supported by your pals, and even then you've got to be conscious of all that's going on around you – you have to be ready to fight birdy style. There's none of this high-street stuff used in prison fighting, you can't back down; you can't let them see that you're weak minded;

you don't go running to screws saying, 'Please, sir, that man's just hit me.'

I had a fight with this kid. Mark was threatening this kid with a bed leg and I was just sat there in this four-bedded dorm, which was full. It was a bit different to the 28-bedded dorms when I was last there in 1984–85. I don't know what came over me; I only had three weeks to go for my first Rudgate home leave. I just dived off the bed. This geezer was about 6-foot 2. He was being cocky to Mark so I just ragged him down and bit the top of his lug off. I don't know what made me do it … just bit the top off.

The geezer went running to the wing office. There was a trail of claret from the dorm leading to the office, but the screws didn't turn up like I thought they would. The next morning I'm up and off to work in the laundry. My jacket pockets had an ounce and a half of tack and £180 stuffed in them. The money was from selling the tack and the booze; tack would go for phone-card deals, or you would get baccy and money. The baccy and the telephone cards were being converted to money and this was handed out on a visit, which would pay for the next load of tack, and you would live like a king, that was the whole idea – why make life too hard?

As soon as I got into work I hung my jacket up near to where I was working, as you never knew when you were going to get a spin by the 'burglars' [security], as they were known; they would give you a spin at random. Three screws came for me and took me back to my pad. I knew something was off; naturally, I left my coat hanging. When I was taken back to my pad I was told to pack my kit. I told them to 'fuck off' and told the screws to pack it. I should have packed it myself because when I was able to check it, half of it was missing.

I knew I was being 'shanghaied' or 'ghost trained' as they called it. They went for Mark and he ended up in the next cell to me in the block. I asked Mark what had happened to the stuff in my jacket. It turned out that Mark had banked the tack and stashed the money in his underpants. That's what being good mates was all about. We were ghosted to Lindholme Prison at Hatfield Woodhouse, Doncaster – a fucking horrible jail!

The reason given for us being shipped out was that I was taking photographs in prison. That's a definite no-no in any prison, not unless you get permission and then it's done with their camera, usually a Polaroid-type camera. The argument Mark had with this kid I bit the ear off was about the photographs he had up on his pinboard above his bed.

Every Sunday is pad inspection at Rudgate. One of the screws had clocked them on the board and had said, 'Those photos have been taken here, what are they doing up there?' That's what started the argument, but, give the guy credit, he didn't drop me in it for biting his ear off. That's how it is. Grassing in prison is worse than grassing outside.

So when I was at Lindholme I put in a complaint form and the word came back that I was actually the 'photographer'. Wonder what made them think that? As it happens, there was no evidence of me having taken any photographs, but I've got photographs from every prison I've been inside of. There I was stuck in stinking Lindholme for six months; I saved my VOs [visiting orders] up so I could take up what is called accumulated visits in a more local prison. My plan was, as soon as I got back to the north-east, to make my stay a more permanent one and tell them to fuck off if it meant going back to Lindholme.

In the meantime, I'd put an application in to be transferred to Acklington, the most northerly prison in England. Four days before I was to be transferred for the accumulated visits I'd built up, I was told I had my transfer to Costa Del Acklington approved. By this time Mark had absconded while on a home leave so I was stuck there on my todd.

I was in a dorm of 14 and most of the other cons were Rastafarians. By this time I'd tried coke, heroin, crack. I'd tried everything, and I had a good time down there with the Rastas. The prison was shite but these guys knew how to party and have a good laugh. I got in with a few kids, which made it a bit better and that. I was also on education studying Business Studies – fucking hell, man, I spent six months on a Business Studies course while drugged up; sounds like most of the students around us today, blowing all their grant money on booze and drugs. We did the same inside.

I was put on the national draft for transfer to Acklington, which meant I was transferred to Leeds Jail at Armley; I was stuck there in the dungeons, as I was just classed as another con passing through the system. I bumped into Quincy [Michael Quinn], my old ramraid gang member. He was en route from Acklington down to Lindholme. We were going in opposite directions. Quincy, though, was refused Lindholme because he had some sort of other court appearance or something, so I travelled back up under more secure conditions than when I had moved from Everthorpe to Rudgate.

Quincy was dropped off at Durham Prison while I was weighed off to Holme House Prison at Stockton, Teesside. When I was at Holme House, a 'B' category prison, I asked to see the governor to make an application to stay there and finish off my time. Out of all the prisons I've been in, that type of category prison was the best: the scran was better, the conditions were better, more facilities to occupy your time, cleaner landings, and on top of that Quincy had told me that Acklington was shite. He was telling me that people were getting stabbed this and the other.

I was refused a stay at Holme House, but I knew I could hold my own at Acklington and if it came to fighting birdy style then so be it, they'd better be the ones to watch out, not me! Acklington wasn't that bad and it was just as in any other prison: you kept your nose to the wheel and you got on with it. I worked in the textile shop, putting plenty of hours in. The more hours you put in counted towards extra home leave; every hundred hours meant another extra day on leave – man, did I fucking work!

I was working on those mats that are used on the ships when those big cannons go off and the shell cases fly out of the back; they've got these big mats that they tie the four corners on and then sling them overboard full of empty cases. I put in an extra 500 hours so I was entitled to an extra five days, home leave, and since I'd planned to get married on that leave I was working my balls off.

Nobody wanted to work there, but I found it all right and was looking forward to nine days at home.

It was the Big Day, 14 May 1993, and I was out. It was a Friday morning and by that afternoon I would have made Mandy my wife. This would be our second attempt to be wed, as we'd planned to get married when I was first sentenced and I was banged up in Durham. It's a long story really, but I was a bit of a bastard and like a fool I was seeing another woman on the side when I was free – a typical whoremaster.

I thought I was in a different world when I was in the ramraid gang. We were out all of the time. Very rarely did we hang around our homes. We were clubbing and enjoying life to the full, and if that meant having two women then I was going to have a full life. Mandy's the sort of woman who I felt would always be around for me, but when I was sentenced she found out. I'd told her I was only entitled to one visit per month, but in reality another woman was visiting me. Mandy sussed me out!

The day before we were supposed to be married, the first time that is, I called it off. I was confused, my head was splitting with decisions; I knew I loved Mandy and she was the woman for me. I didn't want to be photographed getting married while wearing handcuffs, even though when it was arranged I knew I'd have to wear handcuffs. Mandy had brought my suit to prison the day before and there I was in a right state – I called it off.

Mandy thought I'd called it off because of this other woman, who had just had a baby by me and had visited me in prison with our baby only days before. Mandy wanted to kill me. Who can blame her? She'd had enough and told me to sling my hook, she wasn't having any of it. I was devastated by it and I knew I'd made the wrong decision. It was gonna be one hell of a job to get her back, but I was gonna try my fucking hardest.

Mandy moved to get away from the familiar

surroundings that reminded her of us being together – she was making a new start in life. I was up against it and I had plenty of time to think about what I'd done to Mandy. She meant the world to me, but crime and monogamous relationships don't seem to mix. After looking back on my lifestyle I could see how fucked up I had become at keeping it all together; the writing had been on the wall for a long time.

I found out Mandy's new telephone number and I plucked up the courage to give her a call. It was make or break time. 'Mandy, will you marry me, please?' I said. I waited for what seemed like forever for her to answer. My heart was beating so fast I thought it was going to explode. 'Fucking hell, Mandy,' I thought to myself, 'come on.' She said that I'd have to stop my messing around if it was to work. When we were together, before I was inside, we didn't have so strong a bond. We weren't married, we had no kids together and I was on a mission of madness. Now all that had changed. We had young Richard, and Mandy had been on the receiving end of it all. Although we were living together, we didn't know each other like we do now.

I'd realised that Mandy had given me my first baby boy and if I wasn't around for him he might turn out like I did, and I wasn't going to let that happen. I needed the stability of a family. Mandy and Richard were my family and I realised this; for the sake of a few extra shags I could have lost it all.

This other woman gave birth nine months after Richard was born, which says it all really. I strayed like a lost sheep; I had no one to tell me to stop being so stupid. None of the lads in the gang were concerned about this. Why should they be? Some of them were worse than me. It was a horrible thing I'd done and I couldn't think of a way out of it all – thank fuck I was in prison. I had been seeing this other woman for a few years, but the test of my mettle was that I've put it all right.

Mandy had given me a week to finish it with this 'other woman'. She gave me this ultimatum on the Monday. Thursday I'd told the other woman it was over and I phoned Mandy on the Friday morning to tell her. That very same day Mandy had seen this woman while out shopping and nothing was even said, but there was a lot of conflict, which I suppose was to be expected.

Author's note: Faggo was a little vague about the rest of the story, but with a little help from people in the area I've managed to piece certain details together so as to give you a fuller picture. The day of Faggo's wedding he got into a fight with this other woman's boyfriend. Faggo was out on licence, had just been married, and there he was in this block of flats fighting this guy and a pit bull. Rumour had it that Faggo's family wanted him to marry this other woman and subsequently none of his family turned up at the wedding.

After speaking with an associate of Faggo's, he says the family said they weren't asked to be at the wedding and, on that basis, no one turned up – a big misunderstanding really. That night Faggo called at his mother's home but he'd been told that she'd gone to this other woman's house, so he made his way there but when he arrived his mother wasn't there. Faggo was talking to this woman, and her guy with his dog arrived on the scene.

Faggo had been to see the child and, as he was putting him down, this woman's boyfriend at that time started fighting. Funnily enough, since then that guy isn't with her any more and I've been told he and Faggo get on well.

When such a story is told to me, I have to be sure on the facts and, sure enough, the story checked out. After quite a bit of legwork I managed to find out that the other woman played a small part in Faggo's life. She's worked in bars around the area and, as far as everything goes, Faggo sees this other child and it's a part of his past that he accepts.

Faggo was uncertain of telling me the facts for fear of causing trouble, and in a small community this would be so, but in reality this story is re-enacted many times over across the country and the consequences of having had these two relationships seems to have settled down.

I intend to leave things as they are without exposing

too much, just as I left things as they were long before Mary Bell (child-killer from Newcastle) was found by the woman who wrote her book, yet I knew Bell was running a sweet shop in Blyth, Northumberland. I could have approached her long before this woman came along and paid her a vast sum for her story. I left it out as I knew it would hurt her victims' families and yet this woman comes along and fucks it all up for a lot of people. I'm not into that, even though I went to the same school Mary Bell went to in the Scotswood area of Newcastle. I found out quite a bit of info that would interest the locals but that's all. So with that it's back to Faggo.

Faggo: I was picked up in a yellow Rolls Royce for my final home leave. The minute Mandy seen it she said to me, 'I'm not getting in that thing.' Mandy called it a banana and she was saying, 'Everyone's looking at it.' As I looked at Mandy my thoughts drifted off to when we first met. I recalled how I'd felt attracted to her. She'd cut me to the bone and I knew I had to have her by my side; even though I'd loved before, there was nothing to compare to this. This other woman didn't have such an effect on me. This was a fairytale ending to it all and words can't describe how I felt about being with my Mandy.

I've been married now for ten years, although we've been together for nearly 20 I'm out now and I can see my two sons grow up. I remember back to when I was only 15 years old and I was in a relationship with a woman. She had two of her own kids; we had a daughter together. God it was all so fast back then. I've done what I've had to do in life and now I'm settled.

We only dance in life for a short while and, even though I wanted that moment to last forever, I knew we'd have to eventually get on with life. We had to say our goodbyes at the end of that home leave and it made my journey back to prison harder still. I remember when I was young, I used to think who would be my love and now I know; Mandy's my day and night, my sky above and my love. Fuck me, we haven't got much but, you know, I wouldn't trade it for anything else so long as I've got Mandy.

My thoughts are now on what we done years ago when we got sentenced. It gives me the impression that everyone used to look up to us for what we done because we used to take the piss out of the police and that was basically it, and nothing could stop us as far as we were concerned. Everybody knows me, really, so I don't know, I think people looked up to us.

That's why I got married. I'm getting on, but I'm happy. (Author's note: Faggo thinks because he's in his 30s that he's getting on.) How can I try to explain to my son when he grows up what I've done? From when I was young I was always told to listen. Doesn't that make you change your life? It changed mine and I went away in the end, drifted off. There are times to make changes and when you're young there's so much you have to go through. All the times that I've cried keeping the things inside that I wanted to let out, well ... all that's changed. Not many people understood.

Ramraiding was sort of all about letting it out. I couldn't keep it in, I had so much to say and it was the only way of saying it. I had to live for the day and let it go. I had to let the demon out, I had to show the world how I felt; the world couldn't see what it was all about though. I had to show what I had in me, show them what I meant; maybe no one can understand that.

There are so many people out there that are living a lie, business executives marrying into business, but I found a hard-headed woman who has taken me for myself. I don't need anyone else. Mandy has made me do my best; she's my hard-headed woman. I know a lot of men are attracted to a lot of pushy women, but they've got no answers when asked what's it all about. Mandy has helped me a lot. I've seen a lot of my pals get women based on how well they do, but there's only one way to find a hard-headed woman in this life and that's to go through hell and see who's still at the other end waiting there for you.

We had all kinds of things as a gang of ramraiders, but true love wasn't one of them. I remember as a kid having warm toast for tea. God, it was the business. How can you have such simplicity in life yet feel so comforted? Ask Mandy, she'll tell you. Now all of my imaginings have passed and my feet are firmly on the ground. I hope others can learn from the experience I've been through.

If I had known the score about drugs when I went to jail, I wouldn't have gone to jail for ramraiding. I wouldn't have been ramraiding, I'd have been selling drugs really, 'cos that's where the money is. I remember Saturday nights, girls and booze, but now it's Sunday, Monday, Tuesday, Wednesday, Thursday, Friday and Saturday night, booze and drugs! The drug culture's changed it all, that's where the money is, in drugs. The jail isn't too heavy and now with cannabis classified as a class C rather than class B drug, it leaves the door open to legalise other 'soft' drugs. Fuck me, the government would make more tax off drug sales than they would out of duty on snout.

Before I went into prison I didn't touch a drug or even drink but soon as I went into prison I tried it all. When you're on steroids and certain drugs, you've got loads of front and just growl at people. I remember when I was inside and on steroids, this kid walked past me on the landing and he said something, I don't even know what it was, but I just turned on him like a dog saying things like, 'Who are you fucking talking to? I'll pull your fucking head off!' You think you can fight ten men! It all depended on what drugs you were taking.

I remember when I was first introduced to smack, it was at Everthorpe. A lot of the junkies were leaving dirty needles lying about and the screws were going mad. They were taking the needles from the prison hospitals or the prison doctor's surgery. Any con working in this area would have access to such needles and for a few ounces of baccy some of them would sell their own mother. I've seen boilers, normally used to heat water up for the wing inmates to fill up their flasks or tea jugs from, being used as makeshift sterilisers. What I've seen is socks filled with needles suspended in the boiling water; we've set about these junkies for doing such things. A clique of us in jail would keep away from the junkies using needles to jack up. OK, we'd be smoking tack and what have you but we wouldn't be responsible for the spread of AIDS amongst inmates.

You'd go down for tea, take the lid off the boiler and see a manky sock filled with needles being sterilised, so you've got to get these junkies off the landing. It's no good going to the screws and grassing on them, we wouldn't do that. You can't have them doing stuff like that; you don't want them anywhere near you. I mean you don't want to be doing time and then going home and dying of AIDS or giving it to your wife so your baby's born with AIDS or HIV, do you? Once I seen this happening in Everthorpe I kept away from the smack, but I always said I'll try every drug in the jail to see what it's like and what effect it has on you.

Drugs fuck the user up. I've seen guys go on a visit and strip the gold from their women to buy a tenner bag. I've seen brand new trainers being swapped for a tenner bag. I've even seen twins who share everything fight and fall out just because one of them's got a tenner bag and said nothing to the other one. One of them's ended up stabbing the other one up the arse just because of this.

I was in Lindholme and there was a kid called Jo-Jo, a big black kid he was, about 6ft 4in and full of muscle. He used to wear a bandanna and carry a walking stick. He used to walk around the exercise yard at six o'clock and it was pitch black on this exercise yard. I was running about with Barry Cheatham so I was all right.

How I met Barry was that I was on the telephone one day and I heard someone say, 'I hate Geordies!' So when I finished my phone call, I approached this guy who I'd heard had been biting other inmates, lips and the likes off. When I met him, he'd served something like 24 years and still had something like five years left before his review. I went up to him and said, 'Look, I'm a Geordie, OK, you might hate us but I'm fucked if I'm going to run around hiding from you.'

I had recalled when a hard guy from Newcastle was looking for me, he was said to be the hardest in the north-east and I heard that he was looking for me – his name was Viv Graham. Viv spotted me when I was out in one of the shopping malls. One of the people he was with pointed me out to him and he approached me. I was with friends and Viv mistook one of my pals for me. I said, 'Viv, here I am, I hear you're looking for me?' He was OK about it and, in fact, we hit it off and parted on happy terms.

So I wasn't going to run away from this Barry Cheatham guy. Barry said to me, 'What are you doing, do you fancy a walk around the exercise yard with me?' So we hit it off and as we were walking there was this big black kid, Jo-Jo. There were different firms scattered about, the Manchester firm, the Liverpool firm, there were Asians, there were Pakistanis, a couple of Geordie firms, Middlesbrough firms, there were different firms – it was a big exercise yard.

As I said, I was also involved with some big Rastafarian firms from Leeds, Halifax and places like that and they were the most feared, fucking brilliant, honest to God. My first night there I was chucked on the induction wing dorm and I was there for two weeks. I'd been spotted by this kid I'd had a rick with in Everthorpe and he turned up at the entrance of this dorm at six o'clock with a small firm for back-up, as he'd been there a while and built up his friendships with these other cons.

This kid said, 'Tell that fucking Geordie to come out!' meaning me, so I went out accompanied by my pal, Mark, from Middlesbrough. I had this metal knife and fork in my pocket, so I was conscious of this and at the ready in case they were needed as I knew there was going to be trouble. This firm was standing there like something out of the Blue Lagoon, caps pulled down and with donkey jackets on.

This Scottish kid who we had chinned in Everthorpe, to his credit, had built up a nice crowd of pals in Lindholme. There were fucking loads of them so I moved to a space where I could start throwing myself about. I looked for the biggest amongst them, as he was my target. He was going to be the first to get his balls filled full with the property of Lindholme Prison – a knife-and-fork set. That's how you fight birdy style, you don't look for the easy target in a crowd. Mr Big is always going to get it and you hit him with your full salvo of cutlery and that will show the other motherfuckers what lies ahead of them. I'd worked my way close to the biggest of them.

The turnout, though, was to ask if I wanted to carry the trouble on from Everthorpe; he said, 'Do you want the trouble carried on or what?' Mark and I indicated that we didn't want to carry the trouble on and to forget about it. Everything was all right, but this Jo-Jo character whacked this kid in the Scottish geezer's group on the head with his walking stick, right across his napper, and boosh. No sooner had this kid gone down than one of the gang had this geezer's pants down, finger up his arse looking for his heroin; that's what it was like, finger up his arse. I thought, 'Fucking mental nutters!'

These Rastafarians I met up with must've been sound sleepers 'cos I recall waking up in the morning and seeing my bed surrounded by shoes and slippers. I could guess what they'd been doing with them because I snore. These kids were saying, 'We'll have to get a dorm change, all that fuckin' snorin', man.' I said, 'Any fucker throws shoes at me, slippers or owt like that, I'll fucking do you'se when you're asleep, you bastards.'

They thought I was a bit raj because I was doing a big sentence and all that and being shipped out of one jail to another. So I got on with them. I was making myself a bucket and I asked a kid for a washing-up bottle and he says, 'You'll want some soap powder.' I said, 'No, man, I'm having a bucket of tack.' He thought I was going to do some washing, so I started cutting the bottom off the plastic container, made a chilm out of some foil, loaded it with rack and set about 'having a bucket'.

After he'd watched me he said, 'Fucking hell, man, Geordie!' Well, he hadn't seen this done before because they were into crack and all that. I said, 'Do you want one?' He had one and he's running around shouting, 'Fire, boss, fire!' We called the screws 'boss', but he was just making on he wanted them; there was smoke coming out of his nose and everywhere.

That night came and we were all locked in the dorm. There's a shower and toilet block at the end of the dorm and the doors were always left open for us. There was a step about six inches high, which meant if it were flooded it wouldn't run into our dorms. What they used to do was turn the hot tap on, leave it running and shut the door. The room soon filled up with steam and so they now had a sauna. When the water level was getting dangerously close to the top of the step, they used to scoop water up with a five-gallon drum and slop it down the toilet. The steam would be rising, the extractor was turned off and it would be like pea soup in that room.

So I'm sitting having a bucket and I lay there chilling out on my bed. I'm looking and I see all of these Rastafarians going in and out just wearing boxer shorts! I'm thinking, 'What's going on here?' I was paranoid to death. This Rastafarian, Clive, comes over and he says, 'Geordie, coming into the sauna?' I thought, 'I fucking know I am.' He must have had an idea of what I was thinking so he said out aloud, 'IT'S A SAUNA, IT'S A SAUNA, COME IN, COME IN!' I thought they were trying to get me in to ride me; with having the bucket and being paranoid to death I was wary. Clive was saying, 'Come on, man, come on!' So I was creeping closer and I had a look around the door and I see them all sitting on little buckets and what have you.

And that's when I tried the crack. They gave me a little jam jar, with a foil on top with elastic bands around. The foil had holes in one side and a little hole on the sucking side so they put the crack over the hole and you've got to burn the crack and suck at the same time. This Clive used to give me tissues loaded with crack; this kid who was in from Wales was saying to me, 'There's about fifty quid's worth of crack there.' Clive used to say, 'Go on, Geordie, that's for you.' I used to give it away as I only tried it the one time, but they thought I was still taking it.

The heroin. I chased the heroin on the foil. I had a go at that about three times and it nearly got me, and I knocked it on the head. Everybody else was taking it so I had a go of it. They said I had to chase it down the foil and then have a tab straight away. It was a nice feeling but you felt sick at the same time. They say when you're sick that's when the buzz kicks in. It was the same with them temies [Temegesic]; they were going berserk for them.

I got a load of MSTs [Morphine Sulphate Tablets] on a visit, 52 MSTs, but I didn't take them and I got a phone card a piece for them. I got 52 phone cards in two days; they reckon they're a bad old tablet. Somebody gave me four P75s, little red tablets they are. I took the four on the Friday teatime; I fell asleep until the Monday morning. I was just getting up and going for a piss and coming back to bed. Monday morning came and I even fell asleep at work all day; these tablets totally wiped me out. I've tried temies. They make you spew up. I just wanted to try them. Everybody was into drugs in one way or another so I just wanted to see what they were going berserk for. Boredom and mental torture made me turn to drugs.

At Acklington I put in for my parole. I got a KB [knock back] for my first application but I was given what they call a 'review'. I was given an eight-month review; I was trying to win my cat 'D' status back so I could go up to Kirklevington in Yarm, Cleveland. That was the place to be if you could get there, but it had a very strict regime; even a sniff of drugs and you were out but the benefits outweighed that sort of thing. You could have a job outside of prison, keep a car there, if you weren't banned from driving like I was, have your own television set and video recorder, go home for the weekend – more like a rest home than a prison.

I was accepted to go there, but because I was awaiting a parole answer I couldn't go. I'd had a home leave and returned, and I was due another home leave. I took that and when I got back to prison I was pulled into the office and was told, 'Do you want the bad news first?'

'What's that?' I said.

'We're moving you off the wing in a couple of weeks' time.'

I said, 'What's the good news?'

'You're going home, you've got parole.'

I was released on 13 December so I was lucky to make it out before Christmas; I'd done just under three years.

People wanted me to do blags with them as a getaway rider on a motorbike, snatches, this, that and the other. But I'd just come out of prison; I had a bairn and that so I didn't want to go back inside. I think that's what changes you – responsibility. I was on the bones of my arse when I got out, not a penny, nothing for weeks.

I felt horrible, horrible, you feel as though everyone's deserted you. Before I went to jail I had all these pals, people tooting their car horns outside; the door never stopped, people would come for me, do this, do that and there'd be loads of us together. All my pals who I'd known for years and years didn't come and see me, although a few stuck by me.

I was walking outside and there were people up ladders. I was really paranoid. I was shouting at these two blokes up ladders, 'Who are you looking at? I'll fucking rive you off the ladder in a minute.' I was losing my blob with them; I thought they were staring at me, watching me. I thought to myself that no fucker had been to see me or anything like that. I was starting to think that they'd thought I was a copper or something. But everybody had changed, I just couldn't see it.

I ended up chuckying tack off somebody. I was getting myself into a hole. I was having to pawn Mandy's gold to pay my cannabis debts off. I just felt that nobody wanted anything to do with me. All but two of my co-accused were out; Quincy was in doing life – he'd murdered a guy, stabbed him in a pub while he was loaded with wobbly eggs [drugs]. I'd lost touch with my other associates over the years I'd spent in prison and we didn't team up again for one last hit like they do in the films. I just felt lost and I was having a hard time.

I was doing things I wouldn't have ever thought I would do. I could have taken an easy option and used my skills for what I was good at, but I didn't. I started getting into the wobbly eggs, didn't I. My life was taken once I started getting into them; I was running around like a fucking lunatic. People were knocking on my door and I'd be chasing them around the streets threatening all sorts of things to them. 'I'll chop you up, you bastards, coming to my fucking door,' I'd be shouting at them. It was daftness, wasn't it?

I've lost trust in people now. Way back then you could trust people a hundred per cent, but these days it's very hard to find someone you can trust. There's that many drugs flying about and, boosh, they're off and telling this to somebody and they in turn go and tell somebody else and soon it's all over the fucking shop. Things get added on. You think ... well, who can you trust?

I was taking the wobbly eggs for depression, as when I got out of jail I was starting to crack up. I used to sit in the house all the time and take them – I needed them. I used to take about two 20s. I was caught with 53 of them by the police. I had to show I needed them and it was with the help of a drugs counsellor from Newcastle that I proved my case.

The police surgeon said that if you took 20s then it would totally wipe you out, but that was a load of shite. I know for a fact I could've taken ten 20s and still have been aware. This woman drug counsellor got up in the dock and said that people addicted to them could take 25 wobbly eggs and they'd still know what they were doing.

Wobbly eggs are little balls of courage or 'charge sheets', which is what I call them. Very dangerous. You can go out and do something and not know you've done it until the next morning. You know exactly what you're doing at the time but once you fall asleep and you wake up you don't know what you've done the night before. I think it makes you more depressed when you're on them so I came off them and came off the tack as well, trying to get my head sorted. It was mainly for the kids and that, so I could be with them and do more with them.

Looking back at my ramraid days, it was all about getting the very best of everything, like the best tracksuits, the best of gold necklaces, the best trainers, nice-looking car, nice motorbikes, just being flash really. To anybody considering doing ramraids, I'd say if there was a lot in it then it's for them to decide what to do, but me personally, I wouldn't do it again, no!

There's other ways to make money – legally. A waste of time it was. It was good at the time because I thought it was a buzz. I used to make money but I'd blow it and run around in a new XR3i done up as an RS Turbo.

At the end I had nothing to show for it apart from a six-year jail sentence, missing my children growing up. I'm not going to jail for nothing, it's as simple as that. Coppers used to come around and look at cars I'd have parked at my door.

One car in particular was a kit car, but it looked like a Ferrari Countach. I'd go out and ask them if they liked it and I'd say it was a Ferrari worth over a hundred grand. I could see them feeling sick over it; they were just bobbies on a few grand a year and here was me running around in a flash car that would have paid their mortgage off a few times over – flash bastard that I was, or so they thought!

I couldn't say prison was of any use to me; look what it did to me, look at the drug culture inside. Now what they've done inside prisons is to make drug testing compulsory, if you refuse then you can have 28 days added on. Tack stays in your system for up to 28 days so they've gone from that to harder drugs that only stay in your system for between one and three days. That's how stupid the people who make the rules are. When tack was the main drug there was less violence inside. Now, though, it's heavy class 'A' drugs – think about it.

Now I get a buzz from playing five-a-side football and working out, without the help of steroids. I couldn't have done this interview a few years ago, I would have been out of my head, but here I am and that's gotta give hope to all of the others who are in the position I was in. I've got a decent motor and a powerful bike, all street legal. I won't even touch the tarmac unless I'm all legal. If I get a pull off the law, I pull over and take it on the chin, not because I'm chicken, but because I know I'm all legal and it's a nice feeling to know you don't need to run.

Now I can watch my children grow up and maybe one day they'll need my help and I'm gonna be around for them – that's a hundred per cent sure thing. My toys-for-boys days are over. Fuck me, I sound like I've grown up, well ... nearly.

CHAPTER NINE

YOU'RE GOING TO JAIL, SON

ANN HAIG'S STATEMENT may, on the surface, appear to have been a damning piece of evidence. But it was, in fact, Joanne Lynne Bewick's subsequent statement to the one in which she made no reply that hammered the nails into the gang's coffin lid. In an interview, which took place at 10.20pm in a police station after she had been arrested, it all came out. Bewick was asked where the scanners were from. 'He [Brian Richardson] bought a new 1,000-channel one from someone who had got it from Comet on hire purchase.' Bewick went on to describe how she was present when a stolen car had goods removed from its boot.

Bewick named Faggo as the driver on a ramraid and indicts Richardson, her boyfriend, as the main man. 'Bri's always first because he wants to get out first ...

they were going out with two Cosworths.' John Hall, now murdered, death from a gunshot wound to his head in 1999, was also named as one of the ramraiders to have become locked in the Berghaus factory. Bewick went on to describe how Richardson had 'a rack full of coats in his hands'. She went on to say, 'Faggo has always been the driver. There were three cars on this job ... Hutton used to ram the warehouses until he got put away.'

She spilled the beans on the lot of them, including how many coats were sold and other details that greatly assisted the police. 'Well, they done what they wanted with them or people used to come from the town. Lenny Conroy used to buy a few of them, Paddy Leonard used to buy a lot off the shelf. They're big gangsters them, like!' Bewick went on to describe how a leather factory in Newcastle had been raided by the gang and gave a full description of the route taken. 'Hang on,' Bewick said, 'he's done that many, I can't remember.'

A cigarette raid on the Metro Centre shopping mall petrol station was mentioned and Mark Wallace was named as a being a gang member who went back twice. It would seem that Bewick had written a list of the raids that included Boots store in Eldon Square, Newcastle. 'They even took places on with security guards; they were just not bothered.' A raid on Marks & Spencer's flagship store at the Metro Centre was described by Bewick. 'That was when Woody was out and they were going berserk. Can you remember that big, long chase they done and Woody's tyre burst? They were going just ramming everywhere, they rammed about eight places in one night, just hitting one place after another, 'cos he came in with a nighty for me, dressing gown and slippers. I'd only been seeing him a month. I'll always remember that, Bri kept the stuff in his coat for me.

'They used to meet on the Coach Road ... two cars used to meet there, the subway going to the Team Valley, it's a pathway, they used to drive under there. That was a getaway if they were getting chased on the Team Valley.'

The police went on to ask Bewick, 'Who used to fix up the buyer?'

Her reply was, 'They know everyone, Billy Robinson, in with all them, and Paddy Leonard.' She went on to give the names of 'Boyle, Quincy, Brian and Faggo' as having done Nisa food store.

'They done that, that's when that man was threatened: "Say what you've seen and I'll blow your kneecaps off." Keith Wylie, I think, said that ... Brian caught his boot. He's got a big scar, he nearly ripped it open,' was Bewick's reply to being asked about a town centre Co-op store being ramraided. In an astonishing claim, Bewick goes on to accuse the ramraiders of being responsible for a drug-related death. 'Do you know that woman that died, she overdosed at Deckham? It was them that supplied the drugs ... it wasn't Brian, it was that Tony Wheatley and Quincy.'

Ann Haig was able to detail people she'd seen with the ramraid gang and in part of her statement she says that she reported an incident to the Gateshead Police Station some six months before the gang were arrested. She goes on to say, 'When they had finished carrying the gear into the house, I went to the phonebox ... and phoned the police. I asked for Gateshead Police Station, and I spoke to a man there. I told him what I had seen but I don't think anybody was sent to the house.' This does away with the idea that the police were as vigilant as was made out.

In another incident, Haig again called the police at 3am after she'd seen from her window what appeared to be a Transit van laden with leather coats. The van was allegedly soon unloaded into one of the ramraiders' mother's home. 'I asked for Gateshead Police Station and told the man what I'd seen. I don't believe that anything was done about my telephone message,' she said. Unbelievable, in that twice she named premises as having alleged stolen goods stored in them and yet again the police appear to have done nothing.

The Gateshead Police, having now appeared to be ignoring such information, must surely act on a third phone call made by Haig some months after, when she'd had her baby, but no! Again they failed to act on another tip-off when Haig said she's phoned Gateshead Police Station to report strange goings-on with electricals being moved from one vehicle into another. Again nothing seems to have been done about her report to the police. Three times the police failed to act on information received and yet a police informer, Christopher Theadorou, who was based in Leyhill Open Prison in 2000, managed to get Whickham Police to do his bidding on false information passed to them just to cause distress to a former girlfriend of his.

Haig went on to say, 'Brian was asked by Quinn, "Were you going to shoot that bloke?" Brian replied, "Aye, I was going to shoot that fucking grasser." The next burglary was at Comet or Curry's.'

When Richardson was eventually arrested, he said of Ann Haig, 'It wasn't fucking me. Just because some lass said I've done it, you're arresting me for that? Everyone's been shagging her.' In keeping with the underworld's code of silence, Faggo and most of the gang made 'no reply' to all questions asked. The burglary case against the ramraid gang collapsed at Gateshead magistrates' court, however, the entire gang were then rearrested and charged with conspiracy, giving the police a second chance.

Some of Haig's statement was suspect in that she

backtracked a number of times, adding certain earlier omissions and changing details to fit in with the scenario. In an outburst at Gateshead magistrates' court, Haig pointed to a solicitor and said that he had bought one of the stolen coats from the ramraiders. The solicitor she pointed to was, in fact, not the named solicitor she had suggested as having bought a Berghaus; her mixed-up facts indicated that her story left a lot to be desired. All for the sake of some missed catalogue payments, this ramraid phenomenon that the police had little power to prevent was halted. Haig and Bewick attributed most of the regional ramraids written off earlier in this book to the gang. Hell hath no fury like a woman scorned!

MORE TITLES BY STEPHEN RICHARDS FROM JOHN BLAKE PUBLISHING

Insanity: My Mad Life
Charles Bronson with Stephen Richards
ISBN: 1844540308
Charles Bronson is the most feared and the most notorious convict in the prison system. Renowned for serial hostage taking and his rooftop sieges, he is a legend in his own lifetime. Yet behind the crime and the craziness, there is a great deal more to Charlie.

The Krays and Me
Charles Bronson with Stephen Richards
ISBN: 1844540421
'Since Ronnie and Reggie died, all I've heard is a load of bollocks! Reggie shot my cat; Ronnie stabbed my uncle Bert 75 times; Reggie ran over my hamster; I'm Ronnie's son; I'm Reggie's daughter. Gutless maggots spreading rumours with their sham stories for sale.'

The Good Prison Guide
Charles Bronson with Stephen Richards
ISBN: 1844540227
Charlie Bronson has taken his 24 years of experience of prison dwelling and condensed it into one handy and comprehensive volume. Moved regularly around the prisons of the British Isles he has sampled all that prison life has to offer, taking in both the historic and pre-historic buildings that comprise Britain's infamous prison system. It's all in here, from the correct way to brew vintage prison 'hooch' and how to keep the screws from finding it, to the indispensable culinary methods required to make prison food edible.

The Lost Girl
Caroline Roberts with Stephen Richards
ISBN: 1843581485
Caroline Roberts is a survivor. Just 16 years old when she was hitchhiking home from a weekend with her boyfriend, she was picked up by two of the most twisted and dangerous people in the country, names that would, years later, become synonymous with pure evil: Fred and Rose West. Unsuspecting, she took a job as a nanny to the Wests. The events that followed were to scar her for the rest of her life.

It's Criminal
James Crosbie with Stephen Richards
ISBN: 1844540596 (Hardback)

Dubbed 'the most dangerous man in Scotland', notorious for his daring bank raids, James Crosbie knew no bounds and no fear when it came to getting what he wanted. Although he has tried to 'go straight' many times, the temptation of scoring that one great haul has been too great to keep him from a life of crime. This is his story.

Born to Fight
Richy Horsley with Stephen Richards
ISBN: 1844540960

Few men are tougher than Richy Horsley. Boxer, street fighter and bouncer. Crazy Horse, as he is better known, is part of the underbelly of the hardman scene. So tough is he, that he has even accepted a challenge from Britain's most dangerous prisoner, Charles Bronson, to be his first boxing opponent upon Bronson's eventual release from prison. As a young man, he channelled his rage into boxing and he became one of the most feared fighters in the land.

Street Warrior
Malcolm Price with Stephen Richards
ISBN: 1904034632

'They surround me and get me in a headlock. Everyone gets a boot in. He lets go and I grab a glass and slice him across the face. A piece of flesh goes flying across the room. "Who else wants a visit to the hospital?" I yell as everything kicks off ...'

Malcolm Price was born to fight. As a child his father made him go and box in the gym. At first he didn't want to, but he soon found he knew how to punch and it wasn't long before 'Pricey' had become a feared and respected figure.

The Taxman
Brian Cockerill with Stephen Richards
ISBN: 1844541347

'I'm not a boxer, I'm not a streetfighter, though neither have the guts to come near me. I'm simply the hardest man you will ever meet.'

Meet Brian Cockerill, otherwise known as 'The Taxman'. At 6ft 4in, with 23 stone of rock solid muscle, his awesome power has made him a truly terrifying force in Britain's underworld.

If the taxman taps you on the shoulder, give him his dues or say your prayers ...

Lost in Care

Jimmy Holland with Stephen Richards

ISBN: 1844541614

Jimmy Holland, the youngest of three brothers, was born into a poverty stricken family that was headed by his father, a chronic drinker and gambler. At two weeks old, his mother abandoned him and he was placed into the care of the anachronistic Scottish Social Work System.

Shifted from pillar to post, Jimmy has spent all but a few months of his life in a maze of children's homes, foster care, young offenders.

Jimmy is now trying to turn his life around from being a state raised hell raiser.

Viv Graham

Stephen Richards

ISBN: 1844541274

Viv Graham's name means many things to many people. A legend in his own lifetime, he worked his way to the very top of the North East's criminal elite until his iron grip on its activities extended to the darkest corner of the underworld. The mere mention of his name would strike dread into the hearts of his enemies and all knew that, if Viv was after you, then hell was coming with him. His frightening capacity for extreme violence was never questioned, and his size and ability to fight enabled him to exert a huge influence on those around him. Stephen Richards peels away the tissue of lies surrounding the life and death of Viv Graham finally telling the brutal and tragic stories of one of gangland's greatest heroes.